The Pioneer Journey
Going West
Goin' to California

BOOKS 1, 2, & 3

Happy Trails
T.E. Watson

Written by T.E. Watson
Illustrations by Steve Ferchaud

Going West/The Pioneer Journey/ Goin' to California
Books 1,2 & 3
Text copyright © 2003-2017 T.E.Watson
All domestic and international copyrights apply.
Going West Cover Illustration and Book Illustrations
Copyright © Steve Ferchaud 2017
Maps Illustrated by Kim Victoria © 2017
All Rights Reserved. Revised Edition

Publisher -Highlands Children's Press an imprint of Heather and Highlands Publishing / Scotland and United States of America.

No part of this publication may be reproduced, stored in a retrieval system, transmitted in any form, or by any form, electronic, mechanical, photocopying, recording, or otherwise, without the written permission of the Publisher Highlands Children's Press and the Author T.E.Watson or the Illustrator Steve Ferchaud.

ISBN(13)   978-1-58478-071-7
ISBN (10)   1-58478-071-1
T.E.Watson - Author
To Contact Email - tew@tewatsononline.com
Web Site -   www.tewatsononline.com
Going West is a factional historical pioneer story set in 1852 as a Minnesota pioneer family make their way to the new land of Califonia as told from the eyes of their twelve year old daughter Katherine Summers.

Printed in the United States of America /First Edition
First Printing 2017

This is for all the hard working folk who pioneered over this land with all their hopes and dreams to make this great country.

T.E. Watson

Contents
Book 1

Chapter 1 Genealogy	1
Chapter 2 The Journey Begins	5
Chapter 3 Gather the Wagons	11
Chapter 4 The Wagon Master	17
Chapter 5 To the River	23
Chapter 6 A Welcomed Night	31
Chapter 7 The Legend of the Great North Woods	37
Chapter 8 The Great Race	45
Chapter 9 The Final Count	51
Chapter 10 Beating the Weather	57
Chapter 11 The Storm	63
Chapter 12 Starting Anew	69
Chapter 13 To the Platte	75
Chapter 14 To Fort Kearney	81
Chapter 15 Meeting the Indians	87
Chapter 16 New Friends	93
Chapter 17 Learning From Others	99
Chapter 18 The Medicine Woman	105
Chapter 19 The Gift	111

Contents

Book 2

Chapter 20	To the Rockies	117
Chapter 21	Gritting Teeth	123
Chapter 22	Halfway Home	129
Chapter 23	Tending the Stings	135
Chapter 24	The Ascent	143
Chapter 25	Tragedy on the Trail	147
Chapter 26	Slower to Silver City	153
Chapter 27	Onward	159
Chapter 28	The Celebrity	165
Chapter 29	The Long Watch	171
Chapter 30	A New Day	177
Chapter 31	A Pleasant Surprise	183
Chapter 32	Wonder of Wonders	189
Chapter 33	Decisions on the Other Side	195
Chapter 34	The Great Nevada Trail	201
Chapter 35	Showdown	207
Chapter 36	The Guide	213
Chapter 37	To Carson City	219
Chapter 38	Water Water Everywhere	225

Contents
Book 3

Chapter 39 Into Carson	235
Chapter 40 The Last Stretch	241
Chapter 41 CALIFORNIA !	247
Chapter 42 Welcome to the New Home	253
Chapter 43 Getting Supplies	259
Chapter 44 A Celebration	265
Chapter 45 Meeting the Feather	271
Chapter 46 Down the Feather River Road	277
Chapter 47 Fighting the Current	283
Chapter 48 Down the Feather	289
Chapter 49 The Watery Trail	295
Chapter 50 Terror In The Canyon	301
Chapter 51 One More Day	307
Chapter 52 The Search for Jacob Summers	313
Chapter 53 On Dry Land	319
Chapter 54 The Miners	325
Chapter 55 Raising the Wagon	331
Chapter 56 Fifty Miles About	337
Chapter 57 M.B.T.M.G.T.	343
Chapter 58 On The Way Home	349
Chapter 59 Goodbye Mr. Biggs	355
Chapter 60 Katey Goes Home	363

Chapter 1- Genealogy

"No, she doesn't!" Jakey said to his sister.

"She does too!" Katie argued back.

" Let's go ask her."

The children argued all the way to the backyard where they found their Grandmother digging in the flower garden.

"Grandma, Jakey said you don't know anything about how our family got here to the ridge. I told him he was wrong."

Jakey said, "You can't know anything about how our family got here. You aren't old enough to know that stuff."

Grandma sat on the garden bench, "Yes, Jakey, I do know how our family got here. I know quite a bit really."

Katie sneered at Jakey, "Told you."

"Alright, that's enough of that. Why all the interest

Chapter 1 - Genealogy

in the family?" Grandma asked.

Katie explained, "Mrs. Ackers gave us an assignment for a long term homework project and said we had to write an essay about our families and how they got here.

She taught us about what heritage is and how each one is different from one another. She called it genealogy."

"What is that?" Jakey asked.

"Let's see how I can explain what genealogy is." Grandma thought for a moment and began.

Katie and Jakey sat on the bench with Grandma in the middle.

"Well, let me first tell you that your great grandma and your great grand uncle are who you are named after. Many years ago, right about the 1850s, 1852 I do believe it was. They lived outside a little town called Garden City. in the state of Minnesota, there was an industry called the lumber industry. It was a great source of making a living for many men and families. The disadvantage about this way of making a living was that it was not safe. Many men lost their lives from falling trees or falls in rough terrain – all sorts of things made cutting trees dangerous. Your great, great grandfather was one of these men who did this. They were called Lumberjacks."

"Within the years of 1848 to1849, gold was discovered in California at a place south of here called Sutter's Mill. The gold rush started there. Soon after gold was discovered up here as well and our gold rush was on."

"Great, great, grandfather had decided he had enough

of cutting trees. He had seen too many of his friends lose their lives to brutally hard work and a living that supplied nothing but scraps for a family to live on.

He made the decision to move out to California and either try his luck in the gold fields, start a farm, or die trying. He wanted the best he could get for his family.

There had to be a better way to make a living without fear of having something fall and maybe kill him."

"But didn't they have to give up everything to get out here?" Katie asked.

"Yeah. Did they come out in covered wagons and have the cavalry escort them to the fort and on the trail have to fight Indians who wanted to take their horses?" Jakey asked.

Grandma replied. "Boy, you watch too much television. Yes, they did some of that, but it was hard times, and yes, they did have to give up everything they had that was not nailed down. Grandfather sold most of what the family had and managed to purchase a team of four oxen and a very ragged and rickety wagon with a torn canvas cover for protection from the sun. That is where the covered wagon comes from, Jakey."

All Jakey said was, "Cool."

"From what it sounds like, Grandma, it wasn't cool at all. They had a very hard time of things. The journey to get here must have been very difficult." Katie said.

Grandma continued, "That is exactly right, Katie.

Our family, as well as many other families who came out here, had it rough. No cars like we have. No refrigerators or air conditioning. Not a lot of extra clothing to change into when the ones they wore got dirty or torn. Usually, only one pair of shoes is all they had. And when the food ran low they could not go to the super market or go to fast food. They had to go hunt or fish for it or dig up grubs and roots, or if they were lucky they would find some berries to pick. And I don't want to forget about what happened when they ran out of water, and they did often.

No, children, it was hard - harder than you will ever know."

Katie said, "Grandma, I knew you knew about the family. Would you tell me more after dinner? I want to take notes this time for my project."

"Sure, Katie. I'll tell you too, Jakey, if you will sit still," Grandma told them. "Now go get washed up for dinner. And I will help your Mom get things ready. Jakey, isn't it your turn to set the table?"

"Aw Grandma," Jakey whined, stopped, and turned and smiled a big ear-to-ear smile.

"Yep, just like your great, great uncle. Remember now, come see me after dinner," Grandma said. "I'll tell you how they started out."

Chapter 2-
The Journey Begins

Dinner was done and it was Jakey's turn to help with the nights' dishes. Katie ran upstairs and grabbed her binder with her folder that held the beginnings of her genealogy project, and on the way down, she almost didn't touch a single stair.

"Grandma?" Katie called out.

"In the kitchen. I am helping Jakey with the dishes. I was going to tell you how your ancestors got started on their way, wasn't I? Let me finish the dishes and I will be right in. Jakey, hand that towel here, please?"

Grandma dried the last of the dishes and wiped down the counter. She told the boy he could come in to hear the wonderful tale of his heritage as well but he must behave and do his best not to fidget.

Katie was sitting in the living room with her pencil

Chapter 2 - The Journey Begins

and paper at the ready, waiting for Grandma.

"Grandma, you said I got my name from my great, great Grandma. Was her name Katie, too?"

"That's right. Her name was actually Katherine Isobel Summers, and she was born in 1840. Springtime, I believe. Born in Minnesota. She had a little brother, Jacob Michael Summers, Jr. He came along a few years after and finally little Emily Ruth Summers a couple of years after him. Their parents were named Jacob and Isobel. They were born around the beginning of the 1800's. To the both of you, they would be your great, great, great grandparents."

"That's a lot of greats," Jakey said.

"Yes, that's right, Jakey. That is a lot of greats, but that is one way of telling how many generations back the family goes. Katie, are you getting all this down?" Grandma asked.

"Oh yes, please keep going," Katie said. She was busy writing as fast as she could, trying her best not to miss any word her grandmother said.

"Grandma, you said before that it took them weeks to get ready to start their trip out here. What did they have to do to get ready?" Katie asked.

"They had to sell pretty much everything they did not need. The story goes they sold their farm, and with the money they got from that, they bought a wagon, a team of oxen and supplies. The wagon was used like your Dad would buy a used car today. I have no idea what condition it was in except it was rickety and needed work to make it usable. The wagon needed to be able to hold the family and all of the belongings they had left, and in many cases hold provisions like extra wagon wheels, extra barrels of water, all the food they could bring that would not spoil too fast. There weren't any fast food places out in the western territories."

Grandma noticed that it was bedtime for the children.

"My goodness, where did the time go. Off to bed you two. More tomorrow, okay Katie?"

"Grandma, one more question. How old was Grandma Katherine when her family started out?"

"She was about… let's see… I think she was your age when they started on the journey to the ridge.

I know this because she was eleven when they started and just turned twelve when they finally got settled."

"That's very important. I want to be able to write my report like Grandma Katherine is telling her story," Katie said.

The children kissed Grandma goodnight and did the same for Mom and Dad, then went to bed.

The night went on. A soft breeze floated in through Katie's bedroom window. It cooled down Katie's room and helped her sleep. Katie had drifted off into a deep sleep and began to dream about the journey her Grandmother was telling, but just as she began to fall into a deep, sleep, Katie heard a voice and something or someone was gently shaking her bed.

"Katie? Katie wake up," the voice said.

"Huh, what?" Katie, half asleep, sat up with her

Chapter 2 - The Journey Begins

blankets pulled over her head. "Who's there? Jakey you better not be playing a prank."

Katie got up the courage to bring the blankets down just a little so she could see who might be there.

Just then, the someone came out from behind the curtains. Katie's eyes could not believe what she was seeing, and quickly went under the blankets once again.

"Hi Katie, my name is Katherine like yours. I was told you want to learn about my family."

Katie knew she was hearing the voice but did not believe it. She rubbed her eyes and right there, standing right next to her bed, she saw a girl about her age in a dress made of a blue gingham patterned material holding what looked like a cloth hat of linen. The girl had blonde hair in long braids, and she looked almost identical to Katie, but a bit taller with a small button nose and almost the same amount of freckles to each side of it.

"You wanted to learn about my family, so I came to help you. Would you like to come with me? They are about to leave for California. You can find out first hand if you would like to come along?"

Katie just sat there with her mouth hanging open and her eyes bugged out, not knowing what to do and not saying a word.

"Come on!" Katherine encouraged. "It will be fun. Take my hand and I'll show you. We have to get going. Papa needs help getting the wagon loaded and we can use extra hands. You can help me with my

Chapter 2 - The Journey Begins

little brother, Jacob. He can be a handful, and sides, it'll be nice to have a friend to talk with on the trail."

Katie rubbed her eyes, gathered her wits and reached out to the girl. Katherine gently took her hand and off they went on a journey that Katie was not about to forget. Katie turned looking around her at everything all she could take in.

As soon as they arrived at the Summers' farm, Katie noticed she was no longer in her pajamas, but in a newly sewn gingham blue dress like Katherine's, with some ankle high shoes with laces that were coated with black wax that went all the way up the shoe and two clumsy, wooden block heels nailed onto the leather soles.

"Katie, don't lose your bonnet. You will need that on the trail," Katherine said.

All Katie could think was *Grandma is not going to believe this.*

Chapter 3-
Gather the Wagons

Katie and Katherine ran down one of the dirt-lined streets of Garden City to the farm just outside of town, and began to help Big Jacob ready the wagon. Little Jake was busy rolling out the extra wagon wheels for the trip. Katherine's mother, Isobel, had her hands full with little sister Emily.

"I am afraid your Ma ain't going to be much help today," Papa said. "Your little sister is ailing. Doc said she might have the croup."

Mother was busy making a poultice for Emily of mustard and lavender to put on her chest to help her breathe easier. It wasn't easy to make and, my lord, it smelled bad. No wonder it helped you breathe easier.

"I want you two to go get the flour sacks from inside the house and don't forget to shake the boll weevils out of the flour bin. We are going to need to bring that along.

We can use it for the hard tack that your Mother is making," Papa told the girls.

"But Papa, hard tack hurts my teeth when I bite into it," Katherine said.

"Stop complaining, young lady, and do as you're told. I know it hurts the teeth, but we are going to need it along the way sometime. We can't bring all the food we have in the house.

It will spoil. Hard tack don't spoil. So get the barrel and clean it out so we at least will have some food that ain't full of bugs. You make the choice. Eat what is spoiled and infested with crawling bugs, or do as you're told." Papa said as he stood with his arms crossed waiting for the answer he knew was already going to come out of Katherine's mouth.

"Yes Papa," she groaned.

Katie asked, "What's hard tack?"

It's sort of a mixture of a bunch of different things. Hard tack is a little corn, and bit of flour and water, some molasses and a bunch of salt. You put it all together in a mix and stir it as best you can until it gets so thick you almost break the stir stick and spoon it out onto a pan.

Then, when it hardens, it gets harder than the hardest candy or even marrow soup bone. It's supposed to last awhile, but it takes some getting used to. It does fill you up and keep you from getting hungry. So, hopefully, we won't run out of food.

Maybe Papa will be able to get some wild game on the trail. Fresh meat is real good and it's better for you anyway. We don't get that very often," Katherine answered.

Jacob Summers was a very proud and determined family man. He wanted to make sure that his brood had the very best he could provide, but he was beginning to doubt if he had made the right decision. He stood back and watched his children and one extra from who knows where, ready the wagon for the journey out of the Minnesota territory, over the Nebraska territories and then the hard part, getting over the Rocky Mountains. He was not prepared to take four children, with one being sickly and all, plus his wife over such an expanse of wilderness. And, who knows? They would probably meet up with Indians.Friendly or not, they would be there just the same.

"Isobel, do you think we are doing the right thing in going to California? The baby is sick and we have a new girl out of the clouds and little Jake is strong, but he can't be able to travel that far," Papa said as he grew more concerned.

Isobel answered, "Jacob I have known you for almost twenty years now and never known you to doubt your own judgment until now. I have come to know your decisions to be pretty well thought out and usually good in the final outcome. No, Husband, I think we should go. I would rather go to California and start fresh with a new spirit, than to stay here and see you be unhappy in the lumber mills. The family will do just fine."

Jacob smiled and gave Isobel a big hug, "Thank you. You are the best wife a man could have."

So, with a new revived eagerness to get on with the journey, Jacob went to help little Jake load the wagon wheels onto the sideboards of the wagon. After a while, Isobel made the supper and the girls helped. They had flour dumplings with fresh chopped chicken.

"You bunch best be getting used to these. I imagine there is going to be a lot of dumplings served on the trail. Eat up. We are leaving at first light. There will be five more wagons meeting us on the Beacon trail. We do not want to miss meeting them. We need to finish up here." Mama said.

The new sunrise came and they loaded up the rest of their clothing and hitched the oxen team to the wagon. Off they went to a new and wondrous land. The day was filled with excitement.

Jake broke into a song he learned at school:

> "Off to California -for to see- for to see-
> We are off to California for to see.
> We are off to California for to see.
> Got my banjo in my lap and hound dog at my feet.
> We are going to California for to see."

Chapter 4-
The Wagon Master

"Come on Sam," Jakie called to his dog. Sam ran as fast as he could and jumped onto the back gate of the wagon.

With his tongue hanging to one side of his mouth Sam looked to the house and lifted a paw as if to wave goodbye to the farm. Mama was tearing up and Papa didn't look back at all.

The only things that held Mama's attention were the lines she held to steer the oxen. Jakie just kept on singing that song of his that soon became very annoying.

"All right, Jakie, that is quite enough of that song now. You hear me?" Mama said. It was long an annoyance to Mama because she had to sit next to Jakie in front of the wagon.

Chapter 4- The Wagon Master

"But it's the only one I know all the way through," Jakie said.

"No sass now. Here, you take the lines for a time. I need to check on Emily. She still is not feeling well. This trip isn't going to be easy for her until she gets better."

Katie and Katherine were in the back of the wagon sitting on a wooden chest preparing blankets for the beds everyone was going to sleep on. Katherine had slept on hard ground before and she did not enjoy it. You never knew when you were going to wake up with a critter in your bedroll.

"Katie, this blanket has a tear in it. Would you hand me the needle and thread, and I'll mend it?" Katherine said.

"You know how to sew by hand?" Katie asked.

"Of course I do. Don't you?"

Katie did not know what to tell her. They did not have sewing machines or know what one was.

"There hand that bone needle to me please. Papa carved that one for me. He said I wouldn't hurt myself if I had one from elk bone. It works pretty well. Kind of bulky though. It makes the holes bigger than the needles Mama uses. Hers are much finer and skinnier. Mama made all these blankets by hand, and most of our clothes too. I don't know what we'd do without Mama," Katherine said.

Isobel overheard what Katherine had said, "Young lady, thank you for those kind words."

"It's true Mama. If it weren't for you, we would not even been born," Katherine said.

Katie thought – *Hum, me too, come to think of it.*

The trail continued on for several more miles and they stopped in Garden City to stock up on supplies and a few things for the wagon from the blacksmith.

In Garden City they met three more wagons with families also going to California. Garden City wasn't a big town. It was a town that depended on the lumber trade, just like Papa said. It was made up of mostly wood buildings, some ramshackle tents, about 6 saloons, two churches and a jail with big bars on the front.

There was a guard standing in front of the jail and two guards in the back and a bench in the middle of it. The funny thing was, it did not have any walls on the sides. The man I asked said they had not arrived yet from the iron works in Saginaw, and when they did they would have themselves one humdinger of a jail house. As long as the rains did not come, or it got too cold and windy, the guards did not mind standing watch like this.

"Isobel, you take the children to the general mercantile and get what you think you are going to need for the trip. Don't forget the powder and shot for the rifle and the bullets for the pistol, oh, and get some wadding for the rifle as well. Can't shoot without the wadding. Jakie, you help your mother. I'm going to meet up with the wagon master at the hotel. I'll be back as soon as I can," Jacob said.

Standing in front of the hotel were six other men and several ladies with children.

"Good afternoon," Jacob said.

"Afternoon," the others greeted.

Chapter 4 - The Wagon Master

"I am lookin' to find the wagon master for the journey to California. Would you know where he is?" Jacob asked.

Walking up the street they saw a man with a brown rancher's hat made from beaver pelt. He was holding the reins of a horse that must have stood seventeen hands if it was at all. He wore a brown buckskin jacket and there were three pack mules filled to the brim with what seemed to be provisions for a long and hard trip.

This man was the wagon master. He dismounted and tied his horse and mules to the hitching post. He must have stood six foot, or more. He was broad shouldered and tall, with a bushy, but not long, brown beard.

And from what we could tell from his leathery hands, he was a hard working man.

"Good afternoon everyone. I take it you are part of the group that is going to California? I am the wagon master for this trip. I will do the very best I can to help get you to your destinations safe and sound. My name is Biggs. Gridley Biggs. I have been guiding folks along the California trails for over five year now and never lost a soul. You all brought the agreed on funds for my services?" he asked.

Each head of household handed over a twenty dollar gold piece to Mr. Biggs. That was more than half a years wages for most of the folks.

"Thank you kindly. Now we will be on the way just as soon as you are all settled in and have the supplies you need for your families. We will be hooking up with four more wagons in Winnebago, and then six more in Westfield, Iowa," Mr. Biggs explained" Gather round gentlemen. Let me show you the route we we'll be travelin'.

He unrolled a map of the route the wagons were going to take, and plotted out the trail for each of the men. "I figure we are going to cover twenty mile a day. Maybe less, maybe more. It's rough territory we have to go through; some deep rivers to cross. I hope you folks can steer your rigs through that kind of water.

I am not going to lie to you. This is not going to be an easy ride. So, if any of you are having second thoughts, you best be on your way back where you came from. I don't mean to turn you away from the idea of new opportunity in California; it is a beautiful place to raise a family.

Just so's you understand this journey is long and miserable. I am going to call upon each of you men and ladies to use your God given talents and abilities.

We are going to need your help on the trail. So I hope you are willing to help each other." The men nodded their heads yes.

The wagon master looked around to see if there were any families retreating from the idea. These families were goong no mater what. There was now way the could exactly go back home. Al of them sold their homes and there was nothing to go back to, unless of course they wanted to deal with the bank. No, they were goin' to California and that was that.

"Well, I don't see anyone turning back. Let's get on then."

Chapter 4 - The Wagon Master

The wagons were loaded up. The pack animals and the teams were hitched and when all the supplies in the wagons were readied to go, they all lined up. Even the farm stock that many of the families brought along were tethered to the back of each wagon.

There were goats, cows, a couple of pigs, and all of them waited to trod along with the wagons all the long way to California.I did not know how all these animals were going to make the two thousand mile trip. I guess all of us including the livestock was about to go on the journey of a lifetime.

The wagon master took the point position and called out, "Wagons ho!"

Chapter 5-
To the River

The wagons were lined up in a single file formation and each was packed to the brim. Supplies were on the sideboards, inside the wagons, and even on the extra pack animals that a few of the families brought.

Two of the men had backpacks, and they were full as well. Water barrels were braced on special brackets and rigs off the back of each of the wagons, so they didn't break off or spill too much of what was to prove to be a very special liquid.

One family, the Samuelson's, had six children and even more livestock that followed behind their wagon and a few that just wandered about the trail. A few of

Chapter 5 - To the River

the boys shepherded the roaming animals and kept gathering them to keep the close to the wagons. You just never knew when a mountain lion or a bear was going to pop out and steal one of the livestock. Along the trail the extra livestock would come in handy for that one large family,considering they had so many mouths to feed.

One of the other wagons was full of furniture that was real old. The elderly man and wife called them heirlooms. They said it was from their family. They brought it all over from England just before the Revolutionary War. The furniture belonged to their parents back in the late 1700's.

They kept their hopes up by singing and saying a lot of prayers. They were the most prayerful couple we would ever know. The man came over when he was little with his parents. His wife was born here in Massachusetts, she said. They were on the way to California to be with their children who had already made the journey last year.

Their oldest boy brought his family over the trail just like we are doing. He wrote them letters telling them how beautiful it was in California. The old couple told me how he described the land and how the people are just like us. All sorts of people from all over the world have traveled to California.

Most of them went to California by merchant ship, but many, just like we are doing, went to California by wagon train, and many of them

Chapter 5 - To the River

got there by whatever means they could afford. Some of them even traveled by steamboat, and then by horseback, walking, and then hitching a ride with a wagon group. Some even made the trip on the backs of mules. That is a hard seat to sit for that long. Papa told us that the one thing they all have in common is that they all have hopes that the new life in California will make things better for each of them. Before long, a few days and cold nights went by and I never knew how much I would miss my quilt, and my feather bed and pillow before now. Finally the small wagon train made it all the way to Winnebago in southern Minnesota.

Mr. Biggs made a hand signal and called out to slow the wagons.

"Wagons ho!" He dismounted and looked out ahead. The wagons came to a stop and Mr. Biggs asked everyone to gather round cause he had to speak to us.

"Ladies and gentlemen, up ahead we have our first big obstacle of the trail. This will be a good test for those of you who have never forded a river before. The Blue Earth River is up ahead about two miles and you, your families, and your teams need to be ready to navigate some fast water. This is the shallowest part of the river, so this makes this part of it the easiest to cross.

Mama sighed real big, and she and the other women looked a little worried.

This was the scariest two miles we had ever traveled. None of us knew what to expect. We waited to find out what to do.

This wasn't like the streams we had back home, and none of us had to cross the big river the lumber mills used to transport the logs they felled.

"Papa how are we going to get crossed the river? You aren't going to leave us behind are you?" Jakie asked.

Mama said, "Girls, place all the blankets and everything that you can gather that is inside the wagon and get it to the highest spot you can find. It will take a long time to dry everything out if it gets wet. Nightfall is a short time off and I don't want any of us catching cold from sleeping under soaked blankets and bedrolls.

We did as Mama told us and put up as much as we could, where the water would not get to it. That was not an easy task. We did not have much room in the wagon to begin with.

"Mama what about the food?" Katherine asked.

"Take as much flour out of the barrel and put it in the big jars the hard tack is in. It will be alright if they are mixed. When you run out of jars put it in the preserves boxes and then stack them all up. Put the empty boxes on the bottom; just make sure you can get every bit of food you can, as high as you can. I am sure we will be alright when we get to the river."

Two miles does not take very long to travel when your worried. We soon arrived at the bank of the Blue Earth River.

How were we going to get across this water with

Chapter 5 - To the River

all these wagons? And what about the pack teams and the hitched teams? Were they going to make it? We were soon to find out.

"Papa what about all the livestock that people brought along? What's going to happen to the animals? Goats and pigs don't swim."

"Don't you worry, daughter. I am sure their people will make sure they are alright." Jacob said.

Mr. Biggs called us together one last time before crossing.

"Alright everyone, it isn't a fast river, so just make sure your teams don't stall in the middle. Some animals get spooked and will just plain stop if they aren't driven steady.

So get everything secured and say your prayers. We are going one at a time. I will guide you across to help you see where you're going. Just let me know who's going to be the first. We don't have all day. Night is coming and we are losing daylight."

Our wagon was the first to go. Our supplies were tied down and we already said our prayers.

Papa took the lines of the wagon. Mama held Emily, and Jakie held on tight to the seat while Katie and I held on to the wagon frame tried to stay as dry as we could.

Our oxen team and wagon went into the water first. Mr. Biggs guided Papa as he said he would.

We all watched nervously as the wagon went deeper into the river. We saw the water rise higher along the wheels and begin to make its way into the wagon.

Suddenly we stopped. One of the wheels had become stuck in the rocks and sand on the river bottom. The wagon began to shake with the flow of the river. The water became even higher and was starting to flow through the bottom of the wagon. Fast!

"Papa!"

Chapter 5 - To the River

Chapter 6-
A Welcomed Night

The wagon tilted to one side almost tipping over. The oxen were lowing, fearful they were going to be lost in current of the river. Papa gave Mama the lines and jumped into the water with the ox whip in one hand. As best Papa could, he grabbed on for dear life to the oxen harness. He was waist high in water. The rushing water made him lose his balance and he went under just for a moment. Jacob surfaced from under the cold and rushing water and after he regained his footing, he gave the oxen a great swat with the whip and, with the help of Mama, got the team moving swiftly forward to the dry bank on the other side.

Papa trudged up the riverbank and bent over to catch his breath. Needless to say he was sopping wet.

Chapter 6- A Welcomed Night

"Is everyone all right? Isobel, you are some kind of woman with you holding the baby and steering the team. That was a true blessing. I don't have any doubts now we are going to make it to California."

Baby sister Emily was crying and so was Jakie. Katherine and Katie weren't in the best of shape either. They were pretty shook up. And Mama, well Mama would never have let on how shook up and shivery she was. She had to be strong for Papa and the young ones. Isobel Summers looked around to see if the girls were allright.

"Girls, I don't know how I did that. I guess the good Lord had the angels looking after us."

She just took a deep breath, sighed, and regained some composure. She gently gave Emily to Katherine and carefully climbed down off the wagon to help Papa.

All the kids stayed near the wagon. Katherine held Emily, Katie held Jakie's hand and helped him calm down. He was shaking something fierce. He was wet from his pants waist down and his boots were sopping inside and out. Mama said to get him out of those wet clothes and get him warmed up.

"Mama you know what I would like from now on?" Jakie asked.

"What's that, my son?"

" Mama I want to be called Jake, Jakie is for little boys. After what we just went through, I don't think I am a little boy anymore."

Mama thought about his request for a small moment and said," That sounds just fine Jake. Shall I tell your Pa?"

"No I want to tell him. Okay?"

"That sounds fine but let's get the wagon up the bank and get dried out for the evening first."

Chapter 6- A Welcomed Night

The Summers family drove the wagon up the bank and found a spot for the wagon train to camp for a few days.

The couple with the antique furniture had a little difficulty getting across and so did the others in the wagon train, but all of there supplies got soaked and so did most of the people.

Wagon master Biggs told everyone they were going to have to rest for a few days, take stock of their supplies and provisions, and make sure nothing was lost. The wagons all got to the camp spot well up the bank and lined up in a circle for protection.

Some of the men went hunting for fresh meat. Jake found five good size trout fish in the wagon and gave them to Mama for the fry pan. Some of the others found fish in their wagons too. There was going to be plenty to eat for everyone.

Jake looked funny running around in his long johns, but then so did all of the other boys who had to get dry. The young ladies of the train did not have that luxury.

They had to stay wet for a time and try to find some dry clothing that had not fallen victim to the rivers current. You could hear the ouches and an occasional curse word from the men from stepping on thorns, pebbles while having to walk around barefooted on account of their boots, and shoes being soaked.

After a while the men who went hunting came back with some fresh game. A few rabbits and some game birds were going to be the evening's meal. This took a while to prepare, so while dinner was being fixed for the families of the train, sleeping spots in front of each wagon were being cleared.

It was going to be a very busy evening. The ladies cooked while the men made sure nothing was broken.

Going West/ Goin to California

Chapter 6 - A Welcomed Night

The children who could help, unloaded each wagon of everything that couldn't be busted up or gotten into by critters. The children got the miserable job of cleanup, at least for the children who were capable of helping with the cleanup. There were a considerable number of children who were too young to do much of anything.

Dinnertime came. The meal was fit for a king. With the fish and the game, some berries and some of the corn and other vegetables that had been brought, it truly was a supper to remember.

Things quieted down after dinner. The women were preparing the beds for their families, and the children were playing. As for and the men, the men were sitting around the campfire smoking their pipes and cigars. Some just dozed off. We could all hear them snoring from the other side of the camp.

The best time came when Papa started to tell one of his tall tales as he called them. His favorite was one he told of a giant who helped him many times in the logging camps. He told us this giant stood eight foot seven inches and could handle an axe like a sword in battle.

He could bring a tree down in one swing and could clear a patch of trees in one hour. The best part of the story was about this great hairy black ox he kept along for company.

Papa began to tell the story to the camp…

Chapter 7-
The Legend of the Great North Woods

Papa called out for everyone to gather round the campfire and get cozied in. The citizens of the wagon train, including Mr. Biggs, sat round the fire with blankets and bedrolls.

One man brought a guitar, and one brought a harmonica, and one even brought out a fiddle, just in case they happened to break out in song, so we could all have a country dance. The music would add a little flavor to the story, as Papa put it.

Papa began the tall tale …

– Not so long ago, just a few months if it was a day, I had the most pleasurable experience of working with the most unusual of gentleman.

He was not, as we say, "short in the saddle" – he was

Chapter 7 - The Legend of the Great North Woods

quite the opposite. This man stood some eight feet seven inches tall, wore a great red plaid flannel shirt and suspenders to hold up his huge trousers. On the top of his head, he wore a red hat to keep his head warm that matched his red beard, and in the other direction, on his feet, he wore a pair of the most rugged, and considered to be the best loggers hobnailed boots I have ever seen.

We all asked him where he purchased those boots, as we all ,very much, would have liked a pair for ourselves.

He told us that a crazy, but kindly woman he knew in Nova Scotia, Canada, had made them special boots for him, and she was only going to charge him enough cut logs for one log cabin and a barn, so she could have a place of her own to live and place to keep her livestock.

– Well, Big John MacKaskill, that was his name, being the gentleman that he was, kept his word.

He picked up his double edged logging axe and went to swinging. He found a great grove of Douglas Fir and pine trees, and in a short time, and with each swipe of that sharp axe, he cut down enough trees to make that cabin and the barn. Big John, with the woman's instruction, proceeded to construct the most wonderful log cabin anyone had ever seen in those parts. Oh and the barn! That barn was so large, it looked like Noah's ark. You could have put two of every type of animal on earth in that barn; even though the woman only wanted to put her chickens,

Chapter 7 - The Legend of the Great North Woods

cows and a few sheep in it.

– The woman thanked John for all his hard work and he thanked her for the fine loggers boots. They both waved goodbye and the big man went on his way.

– It was a few weeks after, I am guessin', Big John arrived in our logging camp. The word must have followed him of what he'd done for the woman, cause a stranger came into camp driving a wagon with the oddest contraption we had ever seen.

– It had a smokestack like that of a steam engine, a whole lot of gears, and it was put together with special bolts and drive arms to help drive the wheels that made the cutters go.

"Cutters?" the children asked.

Jacob Summers continued his tale.

– The cutters were at the front of the machine and it held a sort of axe with six blades, as big as John's was, if not bigger.

"Mr. Summers where was John? Did he see the machine in the camp?" one of the boys asked.

– Big John was away in another area doing what he did best; cutting down trees. He was cutting and stacking, stacking and cutting. One of the men from the camp went to tell Big John the word of what had arrived in the camp and that the man who operated it was waiting for him with a proposal. This raised John's curiosity.

So he picked up the man who delivered the message, put him in his shirt pocket and ran back to camp. You can just imagine what the man in John's pocket felt like. His insides must have been turned upside down and inside out like fresh churned butter.

– When they got back to camp, John stopped dead in his tracks and the man he was transporting flew out of his pocket and landed in a mud puddle bottom first.

"Sorry Shorty," John said.

– Big John took off his cap and scratched his head. Then he rubbed his hands over his beard and then rubbed the back of his neck, all the time wondering. what this thing was supposed to be. It was nothing like anyone had seen before.

"I have heard of these new fangled tree cutters in the North Country, but I have never seen one 'til now. Where's the little man who operates this beast?" Big John asked.

"I am right here. You must be Mr. MacKaskill, am I right?" The man answered.

– John nodded his head, yes, with his large arms crossed in front of him, waiting to hear what the man had to say.

"I understand you have a proposal for me," John said.

"Mr. MacKaskill I will get right to the point. My steam logging apparatus can cut down trees quicker than any logger in these woods. And that is a fact."

– When John heard the little man boast in that great way, it made his blood boil.

"Now you listen here, I am the fastest logger in these woods and no machine is going to ever beat me or any one of us here in this camp! SO, you take your contraption and skedaddle," John told the man.

The logging camp was filled with a great loud cheer.

The man continued to sweeten John's curiosity.

"Yes I've heard of your great ability with an axe and how you not only cut the trees but built the house and a barn for a crazy lady in Canada not too long ago. Word got around that you were the man to see about what I have to propose. So if you are at all interested, I will tell you. It has a great benefit for all the men of the camp. But if you're not interested I will take my so called contraption and leave."

– The little man was right. He did get to the curiosity of both John and the rest of the camp.

CHAPTER 7 - THE LEGEND OF THE GREAT NORTH WOODS

Chapter 8-
The Great Race

Well, Big John rubbed his beard with more curiosity.

"Okay little man, let's hear what you have to say."

Big John got eye to eye with the character. He stood so close to the man, the little huckster had to bend over backward.

"Whoa, now hold on there. What I have to propose to you all is this. My steam powered locomotive automatic tree falling contraption can fell as many or more trees than you can in one hour, and I won't even break a drop of sweat."

Chapter 8- The Great Race

The little man said this with a confidence that was annoying to Big John.

"I am here to prove it by challenging you, Big John MacKaskill, to a race to prove to you that the future of logging is here!"

– A loud gasp went through the crowd, and an even louder

"What?" came out of Big John.

John could not help but laugh a hardy out loud laugh. All the men in the camp were laughing as well. Big John stood as straight and tall as he could and placed his axe on his shoulder. He did not have to think about it.

"You are challenging me to a race with that machine, this thing that's supposed to put us all out of work? How is this going to benefit us like you said it would?" The man continued on.

"If you win, I will go away and all the trees that I fell with my machine you keep, and I tear up the plans and you keep the machine to destroy. Most of all, you men keep your jobs and your livelihood for your families. But if my machine wins…"

The little man looked around at the crowd of men of the camp,

" YOU, MR. BIG JOHN MACKASKILL, MUST QUIT LOGGING FOREVER!"

Needless to say, this just made Big John even more determined to prove to the little man and his machine wrong. To have the gall and audacity to say that a machine can do the work of 50 men quicker

Going West/ Goin to California

Chapter 8- The Great Race

and do more of it, well, that was the final straw.

Big John yelled out. "YOU'RE ON!"

The big man went off to sharpen his axe to a razors edge.

Several of the men went to see why this machine was supposed to be so special. They looked it up and down. They saw it was made of bolts and metal with twelve wagon wheels for stability, doubled up toward the back of the contraption. In the front was this sort of swinging arm that held a type of cutter that sort of looked like Big John's double bladed axe, only it was like six axes in one. They all looked at each other in disbelief and told themselves that there was absolutely no possible way that this steam powered locomotion automatic tree falling contraption could ever take down as many trees as they could in one hours time. The only being in the whole of the northern territory that could do that was Big John and they all had their hopes set high on him beating that machine.

The men went to Big John and told him what they had found out and what was, in their opinion, an opportunity to make the little man eat crow.

"You have nothing to worry about Big John." Shorty said.

"Yeah, that's right, Big John. It's too big and bulky to move as fast as you," String bean said.

"We looked at it from top to bottom, and we all decided that there is just no feasibles that there contraption can out cut any of us, including the cook," Smithers said.

Big John felt extra confident, now that he heard those words of encouragement.

"You men don't worry at all now. I will beat that cutter and then you all can make blades for new knives from it, or better yet a large new bath tub for hot baths for the lot of you," Big John said.

Big John readied his axe. He even polished the blade and smoothed out any splinters on the handle just for luck, not that he needed any.

The little man with his machine steered the contraption to the starting line at the edge of a great giant grove of fir trees where both the machine and Big John were to compete.

Big John spit on his hands to get a bit more grip for the axe handle and positioned it as if he was in mid swing. The man was busily getting his machine started. He threw logs in the burner and poured gallons of water in the boiler and was having the most difficult of times getting the fire in the boiler to catch.

One of the men in camp called out the conditions of the race.

"From the time the clock is straight at the hour to one hour after exactly, this race of man against machine will commence. No man in the camp shall interfere with either the contraption or help Big John in any way whatsoever. We will count the logs in the line of the machine and then we will count the logs in Big John's line at that time to see who the winner is. Is that clear to everyone?"

Everyone nodded their heads yes in agreement.

Chapter 8 - The Great Race

The race was about to start. The little man was still having problems and Big John was more than ready. He gave a thumbs up and waited to hear the starters shotgun begin the race.

This was it. The starter called out and raised his rifle in the air. "On your mark, get set."

BOOM!

Big John was off in an instant. The machine was still getting started. But with a great crank of the handle, it finally started and had a one hundred yard gap to catch up. Big John was in the lead and logs were piling up with each swing of his axe.

Chapter 9-
The Final Count

The race was on. A loud cheer from the camp was heard for miles. This brought men from other lumber camps by the hundreds to see what the racket was about.

"Big John is racing this here little man that says he can cut down more trees in an hour with that there contraption than Big John can." Shorty said. "If the contraption beats Big John, he has to quit logging forever."

It was half past the hour, and logs were piling up. higher and higher. The two contestants were cutting logs so fast the men who were stacking them could not keep up. The newfangled steam powered locomotion automatic tree felling contraption was felling trees to the left and to the right and left

Chapter 9 - The Final Count

nothing behind in it's trail. Big John was still swinging his mighty axe with ease and with every swing trees fell beside him as if they were bowing to a king. Only minutes to go, then seconds. The camp and every single soul traveled right behind Big John and the newfangled steam powered locomotion tree feeling contraption.

Three, two, one, Bang! The pistol was fired once more to signal the end of the contest.

"Alright, gentlemen the contest is over! You turn that there machine off. Big John you set your axe down," the starter judge told them. "We will now count every single solitary log that was cut by the newfangled steam powered locomotion automatic tree felling contraption. And then we will do the same for Big John's trees."

This was going to take days, and require more than just a few men to count the logs. Both of the combatants had cut down so many logs that each stack of logs was so high it was impossible to see the very top. In fact it was so high that it blocked out the sun.

So, in the dark of that day and the rest of that week, all the men counted, and counted, and then counted some more. Then, by the end of the weekend, they finally counted every log on both stacks.

The final tally was written down and handed to the Starter Judge. The results were so close, the judge asked, "Are you absolutely sure about this?

You all counted each one, all the way to the top of

each stack? Everyone of you?"

The men took off their hats and nodded yes.

"Are you sure Shorty? You can't count passed twelve ciphers."

Shorty smiled proudly and said, "That's all I counted was twelve logs. And I did a right fair job too. If I do say so myself."

Smithers said, "We helped him after the twelfth log."

All the men watched the judge in anticipation while he examined and double-checked the findings as best he could.

The judge walked over to the stacks of logs and looked straight up at both of them, then he perused the tally sheet once again, just to be as sure as he could. He took out his handkerchief, scratched his head, and the wiped the sweat from the back of his neck with the kerchief.

"Tisk, Tisk, Tisk," was all the judge could say. He took a deep breath and let out an even deeper sigh.

"Everyone gather round. I am about to announce the final results of the race!" he announced.

The men crowded around in a circle. Big John and the little man with the newfangled steam powered locomotion automatic tree felling contraption stood in front of the log stack they had cut.

The judge stood with the tally paper in his hand and both of them to each side. He looked up at Big John and then he looked over at the little man grinning ear

Chapter 9 - The Final Count

to ear with a very confident smerk on his face standing next to his contraption.

The men were getting restless.

"Well what are the results? How long you gonna make us wait?" a few of them shouted.

Big John was standing very proudly with his axe across his shoulder and leaning against his stack. The little man was standing with his fingers in his lapels leaning against his machine, with an ear-to-ear grin, smoking a big cigar. The judge cleared his throat with an, ahem and a cough.

He took a deep breath and said, "The newfangled steam powered locomotion automatic tree felling contraption cut down three hundred thousand two hundred and five."

The little man stood straight up and brushed off his coat, and kept chewing on that cigar.

The Judge continued with the announcement.

"Big John MacKaskill cut down three hundred thousand two hundred and four."

The machine had beaten Big John by just one log. The crowd could not believe their ears. A loud gasp of surprise went through the camp. The proud smile that had been all over Big John's face was now reduced to a sad frown of disbelief.

Big John took the tally sheet from the judge and said, "Let me see that."

Big John took a look-see and just shook and scratched his head.

He could not understand how that newfangled

Chapter 9 - The Final Count

steam powered locomotion automatic tree felling contraption could have cut more logs than he did.

The crowd became quiet and did not say a word. That is to say, all but the little man.

"Mr. MacKaskill, a deal is a deal!" he reminded.

Big John nodded his head, yes. He dropped his axe from his shoulder, and hung his head, ashamed that he had lost the race and lost so much for the men and friends of the camp. Big John turned away. He could not stand to see the disappointment in the eyes of all the men. He simply walked out of the camp dragging his axe behind him. That was the last time any of us ever saw him.

We did hear about a man who sounded like Big John in Canada way up above the northern territories. We heard that's when he found an unusual pet – a big furry, black ox bull, and that it was named William. It was said they were wrestling one day, as only Big John could do, and that when they landed from throwing each other about, they had made hundreds of great holes in the ground, and when it rained, they formed so many new lakes, that moved in just because they were made by Big John and William.

"Katherine said," Papa are you sure about all that?"

Jacob held up his right hand and said with a sincere look.

"So help me, daughter. Now all you young'uns go to bed. We have chores to do in the morning.

Chapter 10- Beating the Weather

Morning came to the camp. A strange, yet, beautiful, late summer sunset was in the western sky. But, this was morning.

"Sunsets don't come in the morning," Katherine said to herself.

Jacob was helping a few of the others repair a wheel that had been damaged by something while going through the river. Mama was tending sister Emily because she was still ailing from the croup. Jakie tended the team and made sure they had enough grass and water. That was an important job, but Jakie was the best one to do it. Papa had taught him right proper. The oxen trusted Jakie, and so, this was his chore to do everyday. The only part that he could not do was lifting the yokes to harness them up when we hitched the oxen to the wagon.

The camp was buzzing with activity. Some of the other women were cooking; many of the men were reloading wagons. They had to take the supplies down from the wagons to dry out from any water that may have gotten into the crates. They were checking flour barrels and sugar bags. Everyone was checking their clothing, what there was of it, to see if everything had dried out and to see if there were any insects that had come along for the ride.

Wagon wheel axles needed greasing again. That got done almost everyday. The men all got together after suppertime and used the bacon fat and whatever was left in the fry pans and bean pots to use as grease.

Papa? Katherine asked, "Uncle Eli told me once when he was visiting from the big lake shores that a sailor could tell what the weather was going to be like just by looking at the morning sky. Is that right?"

"Yes, that's right, daughter," Jacob said.

"Well, then he this recited to me:
Red sky at morning,
Sailor take warning.
Red sky at night,
Sailors take delight.
Is that right?" Katherine asked.

"Yes, that's right. Why all this talk about sunsets and skies and such?" Jacob said.

Katherine pointed to the western horizon, and that

was all it took to make the members of the wagon train take notice that a storm was on the way.

"Biggs, where is Mr. Biggs? We need to find shelter right away," one of the men said.

Wagon master Biggs was just coming back when he saw all the commotion in the camp.

"I suppose you saw the sunset this morning," Biggs said.

"Yes, Katherine reminded us of the sailor rhyme," Jacob told him.

"You have quite a smart girl there, Summers. She is right. I went to see how bad it might become, and we need to put some fire under our loads to get to shelter. I know of a spot near the buttes that has abandoned caves that are big enough to hold all of us.

But it will take about six hours to get there once we

Chapter 10 - Beating the Weather

are on the trail again. So let's get going. We will rest there for a few days. That way the wagons will have dried out, and the storm will be long gone. Right now it is headed right for us, and we need to move," the Wagon Master said.

"But, no one has had their breakfast!" one of the ladies protested.

"Ma'am I mean no disrespect, but, that storm doesn't care if we have breakfast or if we don't. We must get to shelter. Just take it along. We can all eat later," Biggs said and went to help the other men.

Katie, Katherine, and Jakie helped each other get the team hitched and harnessed. Mama bundled up Emily to keep her from getting worse. The supplies for our wagon had come through the river pretty well, and our clothing was pretty dry. It had gotten wet from being in the trunk in the back of the wagon while getting stuck in the river.

An hour or so passed and everyone was ready and raring to go. We lined up the wagons and whipped an extra two snaps to the lines and off we went.

We were on the trail for a good two hours when a wind from the north came up and chilled us all to our bones. The dust it brought made it harder to see the trail and made it difficult to breathe, so, it took more time to get to the shelter. That gave the storm more chance to get closer.

The wind was becoming stronger and colder. It blew so hard that one strong gust knocked over the

Samuelson's wagon three up from the Summer's.

The Samuelsons were all right, but now everyone had to help them get their wagon back up and going. Two of the wagons at the back of the train pulled up and made a windbreak to block the wind from making the job of getting the wagon back on its wheels more difficult. Supplies needed reloading and the Samuelson's children need to be calmed. That was a scary time, but they made it without a scratch. The wagon, with everyone's help, was brought upright and was once again on its way.

With each delay, the storm got closer. The shelter seemed to be farther away now than when they all started that morning.

Katherine asked her mother, "Do you suppose Mama that the pilgrims had troubles like these? They were pioneers too, wanting a better life, just like Papa wants for us."

"Yes, child, I suppose they did indeed have troubles. You help me with your little sister now and keep her warm. Take her back inside the wagon and ask Katie to help too.

I am sure she won't mind. Pretty soon, we'll be at the shelter, and I'll tell you more about the pilgrims if you like. We have kin that came with those folk, and from what I understand, it was a grim time, but they held true to their beliefs and hopes and made the best of those scary times and came out of their storm, too. You watch, we will be just fine. Be sure to bundle

Chapter 10 - Beating the Weather

up and stay warm. We don't need you, young'uns catching your death now," Mama said.

Quietly she turned and said a prayer.

"Lord somehow get the beasts to move faster. I have seen slugs crawl quicker in a head wind. Amen"

Chapter 11- The Storm

The wagons continued on the trail to the buttes that Mr. Biggs had told them about. The members of the train were becoming more and more anxious as the storm became closer. It was catching up with them. The teams seemed to become slower with every step. The winds were picking up and the wagon covers were being blown about like the sails on a tall clipper ship. The children were becoming frightened. The grownups were trying their best to get the teams to move faster, but they were spooking and getting harder to control.

Darker and darker the sky became. Dust was flying into everything. It was hard to see. Not even the bandanas the men wore over their faces were keeping the gritty sand that flew like a swarm of locusts, out of their eyes. The storm was on top of us!

Chapter 11 - The Storm

The buttes were not any closer, it seemed, than they were a while ago, but the train kept going. We had to.

Papa yelled out, "Isobel you and the children get inside the wagon and stay there.

I will steer the team. The dust is everywhere. They can't see, and it is getting harder for them to breathe. The Hawkins team has already stopped moving. We may have to stop as well."

Isobel climbed inside the very cramped wagon with the children and made sure they were bundled up, especially little Emily. Katie managed to wrangle out one of the bed mattresses.

"What are you gonna do with the mattress?" Katherine asked.

"Here, Mrs. Summers, you and the rest get underneath it. It will keep us all warm. This will keep the dust out too," Katie said.

Mr. Biggs rode up to the wagon and called out to Jacob, "Only about a mile to go to the buttes and shelter caves. Keep 'em going! Give 'em the whip, if you can! Nothing in the way, so move 'em up. I have to go help the Hawkins. I will catch up. You keep going. Try to keep together!"

Isobel heard the message and took a deep breath then sighed with relief and held the children close under the mattress and the chest of drawers.

Only a mile to go. It was going to be the longest mile they ever traveled. This was not to be the only storm and not the only hard time they were to experience on the trail, and Jacob Summers knew it.

He gave the team the whip and before long they were at the buttes. Mr. Biggs had already gone, helping the Hawkins get their team back on the trail and ran his horse at a gallop back to the buttes to guide each wagon to where they should take the teams.

All the teams were unhitched as quickly as possible and taken to one of the caves at the end of this hill of five caves. This cave was big enough to hold all fourteen teams along with all the other livestock that made the trip, and deep enough to be comfortable so no harm would come to the animals. Without the teams they were stuck. If anything happened to the oxen, who knows what would have happened to them.

The citizens of the train were hauling inside belongings of food and provisions. They did not know how long this was going to be home.

Several of the men were out in the storm gathering firewood for heat and cooking. When they got back, their wives gave them a tongue-lashing. It was almost as if the wives chorused their thoughts in unison:

"You durned fools. You could have been killed out there."

All of them were chastising their husbands while tears ran down their cheeks, and at the same time, they were hugging each other.

One of the men asked. "What is to become of the wagons? I saw two of them blown over and many of the canopies are shredded."

"It looks like were going to be here for a time – isn't

Chapter 11 - The Storm

that right Mr. Biggs?" Jacob asked.

Mr. Biggs said. "Yes, it seems so. But for now, we have made it to safety and we're not too worse for the wear. That reminds me, how are you all on supplies and food stocks? I think after we have seen what the damages are to the wagons and after we make any needed repairs, it will be at least a week before we can get going again. How are the children? Mrs. Summers, how is your little one? Is she getting any better? I know the storm didn't help her condition."

Wagon master Biggs walked out to the cave entrance and leaned against the cave wall and watched the rain and dust come down in a torrent of buckets. They were pouring down on the trail and the wagons, not to mention all the personal belongings that could not be brought inside.

He simply removed his hat, wiped his brow, looked up to the clouds with all its bleak darkness. Then, while standing in all that rain, mud, and windy fury, he pointed skyward and gratefully mouthed the words,

"Thank You."

Chapter 11 - The Storm

Chapter 12- Starting Anew

It rained, and it rained, and it rained. For days, it went on. It seemed it was never going to stop. Mr. Biggs said he didn't think Noah himself had this much rain. But finally, after eight days of solid come-down-in-buckets downpour, it stopped.

The folks struggled to trudge through the shin high mud. The job of now trying to repair and save what provisions they could and save the wagons from the mud holes they were stuck in was not going to be easy.

They had managed to get most of the foodstuffs and perishable items inside the caves when they arrived, but not all of it could be saved. The one blessing was that the water barrels were filled once again. At least the ones that were left out in the storm.

Chapter 12- Starting Anew

"Jacob, this is going to take days, maybe weeks to get everything back to traveling ways. We need to repair the wagons, the animals need feeding and some of the folks inside have turned sickly. Emily isn't any better. The weather is not helping her. We have to get her to somewhere dryer. And the Hawkins family – that poor family's wagon and all their belongings are stuck down the trail apiece. I don't think they got any of their things or, more important, their food supplies out of the wagon," Isobel said in a worrisome tone.

"Wife, it is going to be hard for everyone. I know you're concerned about everything and especially the children, but we must pull together here. Everybody will help each other. You have nothing to worry about. A few men went to help the Hawkins get their rig squared away. Some others are tending the teams. I sent Jakie and a few other boys to look for dry firewood. The children are doing just fine, it looks like. You go tend to Emy and the other folks who are ailing, and make a fire out of what is left of the wood furniture we brought in. That would be a big help to those who are sick. The sooner we have everyone on the trail again, the sooner we can get to the Platte River and get on the way northward," Jacob said.

Isobel went to tend the folk who were sickly and suffering from fever. She wasn't a nurse. She had no formal education in medicine, but she did know how to make poultices and mix wild herbs for colds and such. She asked Katherine and Katie to go find some of the ingredients she knew would make a good tea.

She would take the flowers and herbs, boil them for a time and make a tea that would break any fever. Isobel always thought it was because it tasted so awful that the taste alone chased the sick right out of a person.

On the other hand, it did not smell too good, either. It was a good remedy. She had used it many times when family members were sick before. The one quick thing it did was helping clear the sinus, but that was the only quick thing it did.

A while passed and the boys came back with arms full of firewood. They brought it to Isobel. This was a welcome sight to the folks who were sick. They knew this would provide the needed warmth and the fire to keep the tea brewing. The fire was also going to help dry things out and they might even have clean clothes to wear from being washed with hot water.

Isobel asked a few of the boys to go back out and get as much firewood as they could gather and keep it coming. She told the rest of the boys to ask each of the families if they had a large cooking cauldron or large pot. She had to keep the herb tea boiling in one and the rest would be used to help cook and the cauldrons would be used to wash the clothing. Everyone's clothing was in desperate need of washing. Aside from the mud, the stench from everyone wearing their clothing for days and sometimes weeks was enough to make a person gag. The blankets, the clothing, the bedrolls, even the hats the men wore, must be washed and dried, so she stoked up fires and washed the blankets and clothing outside the cave.

Chapter 12 - Starting Anew

If this was not done, the risk of the fever getting worse and the possibility of cholera increased. Cholera could wipe the whole train out. It was the most dangerous disease of the times and it could spread by unsanitary conditions.

Isobel and two other ladies began the job of boiling gallons of water for all the tasks at hand. They gathered all the blankets and placed them in the cauldrons and added some lye soap. This was sure to clean every spec of dirt out of each and every blanket.

The water was brought to a hot boil.

Then the blankets were stirred about with a strong wooden branch from the woodpile. It was hot, sweaty, hard work, but it was going to do the trick in keeping everyone healthy, so after a good boiling, the blankets were hung outside to dry on the rungs of three of the wagons that had lost their covers.

The day dragged, but the people of the train had done what they found they did the best.

They were becoming a community.

Chapter 12 - Starting Anew

Chapter 13- To the Platte

"The Platte River runs through the entire territory of Nebraska," said Mr. Biggs.

"It flows east to west and then about half way it splits off to the forks of the North and South Platte. It runs for over six hundred miles and travels into the eastern regions of the Wyoming territory. The Indian Territories are a big area and we have to drive the wagons through them as well. We have a few rivers to cross, but the one that is going to be the most time taking is at the Kanesville Ferry Crossing. The ferries can only take one wagon without the team each time the cross. We have seventeen wagons and seventeen teams. This does not include our people. This should

Chapter 13 - To the Platte

take the better part of two days just to cross the Platte to get to the south bank."

" Then, we have to hitch everything up and head south. This will be a long few days. From there we will stop and get supplies in Kanesville. You men remember to have the women pick up trinkets and extra blankets. Those will help us get across the Indian territories. We will need those goods for trading. We will stop at some point to do some hunting for some pelts and fresh meat."

"We'll use the furs for trade as well. We will keep the meat. At least for the time it'll keep without rotting.

This is what we have in front of us. So, I ask you all again are you all still with us?"

Mr. Biggs was done with the plan for the trail the wagon train was going to travel.

The trail we were to take was one that was already plotted and traveled by many of the emigrants that came long before us. This trail was the path to opportunity and a new life. Jacob Summers was smiling now and his face became brighter than it had been in a while. When Isobel heard the news, she felt like dancing.

Little sister Emily finally began to get better. Some of the men took out their guitars and even a mouth harp.

One had a fiddle and another took out a concertina, and everyone stopped right then and there and danced to the music. Even Mr. Biggs

Chapter 13 - To the Platte

danced the feathers to the music. All had a good time.

The music stayed with all of us throughout the day until we came to the ferry crossing at the forks of the Missouri and the Platte rivers. Our work was lined out for us.

It cost each of the families a sizable chunk of money. At ten dollars for each team, wagon, and family, the ferry pilot took us to the opposite bank. The journey over was done on a flatboat guided by ropes rigged on both sides of the boat.

On the other bank there was a man with a two teams, each with six pairs of mules. They helped stabilize the guide ropes and get the flatboat to the landing dock. One team pulled the flatboat, and the other made sure the flatboat stayed straight and didn't get caught in the current and end up down stream. There was another just like it on this side to pull the flatboat back to get another wagon, and then do it all over again.

The oxen were unhitched again so they could go over first. This gave them a chance to get some fresh grass to eat and be watered. A few of the boys went to watch the animals so they didn't wander off.

Daylight was burning away, and the sun was setting, and there were still five more families to cross. The boat pilot suggested that the families go over and take supper with the rest of the train. They would get the remainder of the train over first thing in the morning.

Another morning came and went, and the pilot

did exactly as he said he would. The wagons and the rest of the belongings were already brought to the south bank of the Platte River.

The camp was bustling with activity. Everyone was excited to get on the trail. Some were whistling the songs they played the other day. Another few hours and everyone could get stocked with new supplies and have a chance to stay put in one place for a few days without fear of storm or sickness, and maybe, just maybe, the journey ahead would be a smooth one.

Chapter 13 - To the Platte

Chapter 14-
To Fort Kearney

Mr. Hawkins was finishing grease fatting the wheels to his family's wagon.

A few others spent the morning mending the wagon canvas covers that had been torn in the storm. Some of the older children were busily re-coopering the barrels that had their hoop rings fall off. Everybody knows you just can't hold a barrel together without the hoop rings.

The women were folding bedding and preparing breakfast for their families.

The teams were fed with fresh grass from the fields and watered at the nearby stream.

It was a busy beginning to a hope filled day.

Gridley Biggs went to each of the families and asked if they would soon be ready, and to inspect each of

Chapter 14 - To Fort Kearney

the wagons to make sure they were back together and trail worthy once again. They could ill afford any more delays. All wagons had to be good to go.

Autumn was coming in a few weeks and they had to beat the Rockies and the snows that would be waiting for them if they did not clear the saddle pass.

The day drifted into afternoon and everyone was as ready as they were going to be. Some of the wagons continued on without covers, because they were still being mended. Children were walking with the livestock to make sure they did not wander off.

The teams of oxen were slowly following the wagon ruts that had come before them, and the trail was not getting any drier. The storm dropped more rain than any of them had ever seen in that stretch of time.

"Eight days of rain is a whole lot of water," Jakie said.

"The trail does not look like it is going to dry any time soon. You keep guiding the beasts and we will be fine," Jacob told his son.

Somehow, Jakie had made friends with the team. He seemed to be able to make them step just a little more lively on the trail. The oxen swayed their horns as they plodded along with Jakie kindly tapping their back legs with a willow switch making sure they did not miss one step. At the same time, Jakie would notice flies settling on the animals' backs and he would brush them away to help keep the oxen comfortable.

The flies were so thick at places the people had to cover their faces as if they were in the dust storm once again. The bugs were getting into everything, so the children had one more job to do – keeping the durned things out of the flour, and the rest of the food supplies. Nobody liked to eat maggots. The other insects they had to deal with were the mosquitoes. Trailing along the Platte River, they experienced mosquitoes larger and more plentiful than they ever knew before. The Platte's delta country was filled with standing pockets of rancid, still, water and other places perfect for breeding mosquitoes. This was another reason to keep the bugs off. Mosquitoes carried all sorts of problems. They carried more disease in one bite of their little needle like stinger, and that one sting could and would put

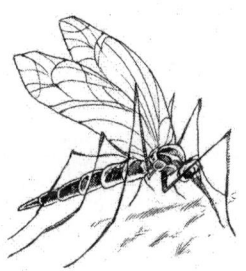

down a full-grown horse. It made life on that region of the Platte interesting and very busy. Everybody had to protect themselves as well as the teams from the critters.

Slap! Slap! Slap! was heard all along the trail as everyone was smacking the bloodsucking troublemakers.

Only time and hope conquered the mosquitoes and fly population and the members survived the bites of the flies and the stings of the mosquitoes worse for the wear. A few red rosy welts rose on arms and faces, but then the itching came.

Chapter 14- To Fort Kearney

"Mama, I don't know what's worse, the bugs or the itching," Katherine said scratching her neck.

"Just try not to scratch the itch, daughter. I will see if we can stop for an hour to prepare some of the wild lavender we brought. That will take the itch away," Isobel said.

She asked Mr. Biggs if it would be all right to rest for a short spell and fix the lavender and clove salve for everyone. Isobel and a few of the other women prepared the salve and brought some to everyone who was bitten. For the children, she put some of these miracle anti-itch ingredients into a few handkerchiefs and tied them around the necks of the smaller children. For the rest of the victims, they dabbed some on each of the bites for as long as the miracle medicine lasted, and the itch on each and every person went away. It stunk, but the itch was gone. They all looked as if they were just getting over a case of the chicken pox but without the side effects of fever and sweats. Some of the men objected to having that stuff put on their skin.

They said it smelled of a fancy saloon. But then, we knew they did not know what they were talking about, being family men and all. Family men did not have reason to venture into establishments of that sort.

Isobel and the others told each sting and bite victim to keep the perfumery, smelly stuff on until they reached Fort Kearney and only then, could they wash it off. The male population of the wagon train could not get there fast enough.

"Who ever heard of a gentleman wearing perfume, even if it does help keep the bugs away?" said Mr. Hawkins.

Soon the train was on the trail once again. Within an hour of sunset, Mr. Biggs was seen riding as fast as he could back to the train.

"Good News, everyone!" he called out. "Fort Kearney is just over the rise. About four more miles and we can sleep safely and ,holy Moses my goodness, you gentlemen can get a bath," Mr. Biggs said with a chuckle. You never saw a happier bunch of men and boys in your life.

At least they were not itching any longer.

Chapter 14 - To Fort Kearney

Chapter 15- Meeting the Indians

By the year 1852, Fort Kearney had been established for some four years to give protection for pioneers heading west along the Oregon Trail. Fort Kearny gave safe shelter for pioneers, Pony Express riders, prospectors and others as they followed the great Platte river road.

The actual fort was only home to about two hundred military men who lived there. The families of those men who also lived there helped keep the fort in good condition and some even farmed to grow the food the fort needed to feed travelers and the people who lived there full time.

Now, since the migration to California and Oregon Territories had begun, this year's crops

Chapter 15 - Meeting the Indians

were getting short and the fort was over burdened. Indians had never attacked it, nor had it been the victim of bad repute by the single soldiers who went into the town of Nebraska City to carouse and spend that month's pay at the saloons. It was a taunt ship as far as military outposts were concerned and Mr. Biggs, who led many pioneer wagons into this sanctuary, knew there would be no trouble for any of the folks under his guidance.

The Summers party was just coming over the rise when Isobel saw the multitude of wagons in six long trail lines just stopped next to one another.

"Mama, there must be a thousand wagons down there. Do you think they are going to California, too? I never knew there were so many wagons in the whole world," Katherine said.

"Papa may we run ahead and...?" Jakie started to ask.

"Not right now. That is a passel of wagons down there. No telling what kind of people are in them and I don't want you children running off until I find out where we are supposed to hitch the wagons with the rest of our party. So you hold your horses for now.

We will be there soon enough," Jacob told the children.

As the wagons came down the trail, the wagon ruts seemed to get deeper with every yard. There was a sea of wagons. Thousands of wagons and folks wanting to make a better future for themselves

Chapter 15 - Meeting the Indians

came through here. It seemed the perfect place to stop and rest. Anyone who wanted to or had a mind to could stop and help the fort do chores and harvest crops.

There was much to do to keep everyone happy and fed.

"Alright. Everyone stay close to the wagon. I will ask Mr. Biggs what we are to do now. Isobel, make sure Jakie minds his self. He is so excited, he might just run off and forget the hide tanning he'll get," said Jacob turning to meet with the other wagons.

"Don't worry dear, the boy will be fine right here," Isobel reassured.

No sooner had his mother told his father he would stay at the wagon, Jakie was off.

Not only did he not stay at the wagon, but he also discovered something he thought they would never see in his lifetime.

On the outskirts of the outpost was a small tribal band of Indians who were ordered to live there on a government reservation. They had a small camp setup to accommodate the members of their community, with teepees to live in, cooking fires for cooking, and tanning racks mounted with fresh game hides.

The Indians were just doing what Indians do. To Jakie's amazement, there were Indian children helping with chores and playing games just like he did back home in Minnesota.

Isobel noticed the boy had slipped away.

"Katherine and Katie, go find that rascal and get his tail end back here. We have chores to do and he needs to do his share. Bring him back quickly, you hear."

The girls ran hither and thither between wagons trying to find that stinker of a little brother. Finally they found him standing wide eyed, staring at the Indian camp.

"Oh my land!" Katherine said. " Jakie, we have to get before they attack us or something,"

"They are not going to attack us. They have chores and stuff to do, just like us. They don't want to attack us," Jakie said back at his sister.

"I think he is right for once, Katherine. They are not going to do anything except live their lives. They don't want any trouble," Katie agreed.

Within an eyes blink, Jakie said to himself, I'm gonna go meet 'em! And he ran off to the camp.

"Katie, what are we going to do?" Katherine asked, quite afraid.

"We're going too," Katie said. "You hold my hand. There is nothing to be afraid of."

They took a deep breath and with a good grip, so they would not to lose each other, called out,

"Jakie, wait! We're coming, too."

Chapter 15 - Meeting the Indians

Chapter 16- New Friends

Katherine and Katie ran after Jakie to stop him before he did something clumsy and started a war. At least, that's what they thought he would do. Being Jakie, he just might. Before they all knew what they had done, they were standing smack dab in the middle of the Indians camp.

Katherine held Katie's hand tighter, and Jakie was turning around in place staring at all the surroundings of the camp.

"Katie, what are we doing in here? They are probably going to cook us or some awful thing like that."

Katie laughed,"They are not going to eat us, you silly girl. What makes you think they are going to do that?"

Chapter 16 - New Friends

"From all the stories I heard back home. Indians are supposed to be heathenistic people with no civility at all," Katherine said.

"They look civil to me," Katie replied. "They are just doing what they normally do, it looks like. They probably don't even notice us being here in the camp.

Besides, this is a small village at a military outpost with soldiers and hundreds of others who are probably watching their every move. You have nothing to worry about, Katherine.

Anyway, it looks like they are doing everyday chores. Getting water, corn grinding, and over there it looks like a woman is tanning a skin. Just everyday chores that's all."

"Well, just don't let go of my hand, alright." Katherine was very careful with every step she took in the camp. She did not want to upset anyone.

Jakie came running back to the girls. He was very excited.

"You gotta come see this, some of the children are playing a game. They are kicking some pig innards. It looks like a bladder. They are trying to get it into a hole at either end of the playing area. Some are kicking it one way and some the other way.

Come on, I want to see if they will let me play. Maybe they will let you two scaredy cats play too," Jakie said, and ran off again.

This was the most excited Jakie had been since they left Garden City.

Going West/ Goin to California

Chapter 16 - New Friends

The girls forgot about what Isobel asked them to do, until they heard Isobel's voice calling.

"Oh my! Mama has come a-looking for us. You get Jakie and bring him back even if you have to hog tie him. I will go and stall Mama. You get back as quick as you can," Katherine said.

Katie ran to get Jakie while Katherine went to see if her mother was upset about them not coming back sooner.

"My land child, where have you been off to? Did you find your brother? Your father is going to be upset at all of us if Jakie isn't back at the wagon soon.

Your papa doesn't know Jakie is gone yet. The men are still meeting with Mr. Biggs and the Fort Commander to see where to lite the wagons for the spell we are here," Isobel said.

"Mama, Katie is bringing Jakie back. We found him playing in the Indian camp," Katherine said breathlessly. "He's alright. He isn't hurt or anything."

Soon Katie came bringing Jakie back to the wagon with a good grip on his arm, almost dragging him back.

She was scolding the boy, holding him with a tight grip, as he struggled along, "You are going to be in so much trouble, Jakie Summers. You taking off like you did put us all in a whole lot of trouble. I am not letting you go until we get back to the wagon. You are staying put even if I have to sit on you. So stop squirming. It will do you no good."

Both Katie and Jakie arrived back at the wagons no worse for the wear.

"Mama, tell her to let go," Jakie said squirming.

"Not until you settle down. You caused a lot of worry for us, young man. When your Father hears of what you did, well, I just don't know," Isobel told the boy.

"Okay I'll stop. I was just playing with the Indian boys. I wasn't hurting anything," Jakie whined.

"No matter. You high tailed it, when we got here and disobeyed your Father. If you are very good, maybe you will get to leave the wagon to play with the rest of the children in the wagon train," Isobel firmly chided him.

Not knowing if they should speak up for fear of getting into trouble for going into the camp as well, Katherine spoke up.

"Mama, we went into the camp, too, but it was only to get Jakie back. The Indians look friendly. They didn't attack us or anything."

An Indian boy walked up to the Summer's wagon.

He surprised them all by speaking English pretty well.

"There you are. Are you coming back to play? We need another player. Kicking Fox went home to help his Father. It would be very good if you can."

Jakie just sat in the wagon, looking at his mother, hoping she would tell him to go ahead, but somehow he knew he wasn't going anywhere for a long while.

Chapter 16 - New Friends

Chapter 17- Learning From Others

After what seemed to be a very long meeting to Jakie, his Father came back to the wagon.

Isobel was rocking Emily and the girls were amusing themselves with some of the other children.

"Well Jacob, where do we set the wagon?" Isobel asked.

Mr. Biggs told us all to bring the wagons around to the north end of the fort entrance and line them up accordingly. There are other wagon parties there and that would be the best spot for our train to locate for the time we are here. Have the children behaved?"

Isobel glanced at Jakie, and Jakie glanced back with a slight glimmer of hope that his mother would

Chapter 17 - Learning From Others

not spill the beans about how he had disobeyed his father and run off.

Isobel acted as if she did not hear Jacob's question right off.

"Well, how have the children been?" Jacob repeated.

"The children have been fine, been here right along. They have been helping get things ready for the settling of the wagon. Isn't that right, Jakie?"

Isobel gave Jakie a look that would have melted ice. Jakie just nodded his head, yes, in agreement. The boy did not quite know what to think of what his Mother just done. She was always so honest with Papa.

"Jakie, you guide the team along side and I will steer the wagon. Girls, would you watch Emily? She has been inside resting on the bedding I set down for her for awhile and needs to get some fresh air."

Isobel piloted the wagon to resting place right where Jacob said to put it.

"Jakie?" Isobel said sternly. "Young man, you are still in trouble, but I do not feel it necessary to upset your father with this issue. You have chores to do, and they are not the type you like doing. Do not run off again, do you hear? You are going to stick to me like flies on molasses this afternoon and you are going to help. Do you understand?"

Jakie hung his head in shame for what he had done. He wanted to say he was sorry.

"But..." he started.

Chapter 17 - Learning From Others

"But nothing. We are in a strange new land with strange new customs and neither you nor I, or anyone else, for that matter, knows what exactly to expect. So, you stick to your P's and Q's and mind when you are told to. Now, you unhitch the team, find them a fresh meadow to feed on, and then come back here. You are going to help unload the wagon. We need to find out what supplies we are out of, " Isobel scolded him something fierce.

But being Jakie, he would disobey his parents again after that.

Shortly after Jakie received that verbal hide tanning, Katie and Katherine came up the road with Emily, each girl holding one of Emily's small two-year-old hands, swinging her gently as they walked. Coming toward them were two Indian girls about the same age with a little girl exactly as Katie and Katherine were doing with Emily.

"Mama look!" Katherine exclaimed. "They are doing the same thing as us. May we go meet them? Maybe we can play and make some new friends? Oh please Mama. We won't be long.

I promise." Katherine begged. "We will take good care of Emily and we won't get into trouble."

Isobel thought briefly and said, "Alright, but you keep an ear out for dinner and keep care of your little sister. Jakie is going to help me today with the wagon chores, aren't you Jakie?"

Jakie just scowled and grumbled and continued to sift through the flour barrel searching for the one thing everyone hated to look for, flour maggots.

The girls glowed with pleasure at the thought of playing with girls their own age. This was going to be a new exciting experience. They played all the time at home with friends from school, but this was a chance to make new friends entirely.

They walked towards the Indian girls almost in a mirrored action. The girls were both swinging their little sister in direct path of one another.

The closer they became, the bigger their smiles grew and happier their faces became.

"Katherine, you don't seem scared of them now. You still think they are going to attack you?" Katie asked.

"What made you think we were going to be attacked, you silly girl?" Katherine said.

One of the Indian girls was holding a doll made from corn husks wrapped around with bead work for a belt. It had two blue beads for eyes and a red one for a nose with a mix of blue and red for its smile.

Katherine saw the doll, turned and gave Emily to Katie, then ran back to the wagon.

Katie, with a look of wonder on her face, wondered what Katherine was doing. In just a few minutes, Katherine came running back to them with one of her dolls. It was dressed in a gingham blue pattern, wearing a sun bonnet. It was a cloth doll with blonde hair and looked like Katherine. Isobel had sewed it for Katherine to play with in times

Chapter 17 - Learning From Others

of quiet and reflection. The doll was very special. Katherine gently reached out and gave the doll to the Indian girl with the corn husk doll.

Katie was still wondering what Katherine was doing.

"That's your favorite doll!" Katie said.

"Never mind. I can make another." Katherine replied.

The Indian girl took the doll and gazed at it with much happiness. Then she hugged Katherine and in turn gave Katherine her corn husk doll.

Katherine had wanted to give the girl her doll as an act of friendship, never expecting to get anything in return.

Smiles beamed from the faces of both girls. They both knew they had made a long life friend.

Chapter 18-
The Medicine Woman

The girls discovered that they both had many things in common, even though they could not speak in the same language. Katie figured out how to sign with her hands to communicate, and soon after Katherine began to understand what Katie was doing. The hand gestures were rough and somewhat crude by Indian standards of hand signing, but they all sort of knew what they were trying to say to each other.

Most of the time, the girls just played and showed each other by tugging on clothing and bringing one another to the thing they were trying to say. That worked pretty well for awhile.

Chapter 18 - The Medicine Woman

Katherine tried to introduce herself to the Indian girls.

"I am Kath-er-ine," she said.

Katie did the same. "I am Kat-ie."

The Indian girls looked curious and tilted their heads to one side, not understanding.

Katherine tried once more, "Katherine, I am Katherine."

Then, she laid her right hand on her chest when she said her name. She told Katie to do the same.

That seemed to go on for hours. Trying to speak with each other was not going to be easy.

Katherine laid her hand on one of the Indian girls' shoulders and then again on her own saying, "Katherine."

Some minutes passed and as if the sun came out in a dark room the Indian girl spoke her name.

"KwoNeShe," which means Dragon Fly.

Katherine smiled and sighed. They had discovered each others names.

Katherine told Dragon Fly the names of Emily and Katie, and KwoNeShe did the same.

But all that did not seem to matter any longer, and they went off to play some more.

Soon they found themselves in front of the tipi of KwoNeShe's family. There they played with the dolls and tried to talk with each other. They had a good time until KwoNeShe's mother was seen running towards the tipi with her one-year-old brother wrapped in a blanket. She was sobbing and crying

Chapter 18 - The Medicine Woman

and saying something in her language.

Without thinking Katherine got up and went inside to see what the matter was.

The baby had been sitting next to some rocks along the bank of a nearby stream, where his mother put him to be safe from the water. She was not aware of what lurked underneath one of the rocks. She was getting water in a jug when she heard a loud cry from the boy and saw a small rattlesnake slithering away.

The Indian woman noticed the two unmistakable bite marks from the snake. The baby cried louder. She scooped him up in the blanket and ran all the way back to the tipi. It was only a matter of minutes before the boy would go into shock and then die. KwoNeShe motioned her fingers like snakebite on the baby to Katherine.

Without hesitation, Katherine burst out of the tipi and ran as fast as she could to get her mother.

Mother can help, Katherine thought, as she ran with every long stride she could muster.

Within seconds Katherine was at the wagon and trying to catch her breath she said, "Mother,

Indian baby – snake bite! Come quick!"

Jacob took Emily, then motioned Isobel to go.

Isobel knew that snakes, whether they be poisonous or not, could do great harm to a baby. She grabbed her medicine pouch that held the lavender and other natural herbal plants she knew would draw poisons out. She ran after Katherine as fast as she could to the tipi and entered.

Isobel knelt down beside the KwoNeShe's mother, who was crying and holding the baby, rocking back and forth to calm the child.

Isobel reached out to the child and his mother held him tighter.

Time was slipping passed. The little one was pale and his joints were stiffening, and place around the bite was swelling, but as long as the boy was crying it was a good sign.

The news spread quickly among the women of all the wagon communities and several came to offer help..

The Indian mother was holding her baby even closer and would not let go, fearful the baby boy was dying.

Mrs. Hawkins knew some sign language and told KwoNeShe what Isobel wanted to do, and Dragon Fly told her mother that Isobel was a medicine woman. Medicine Women are very important people, and after Dragon Fly's mother understood what Isobel was doing, she handed the baby to her.

Carefully, Isobel handed the boy to Mrs. Hawkins. She cradled him in her arms as if he was her own, while Isobel gently slipped the blanket off the child so she could see where the bite was.

While Isobel was tending the injury, the boy's mother began to calm down. Isobel found the bite marks and pinched them together to make the wound start bleeding. This helped clean it out, but

Chapter 18 - The Medicine Woman

the little boy cried even louder.

"Katherine, get some water and bring it here. I must have it to wash the blood away. And if you have a scrap of cloth, I need that too. Tear it off your dress if need be. We can make a new one."

Katherine did as she was told and as fast as she could brought the water and a scrap of her dress.

Isobel ground up the herbs and water together in her small stone mortar and pestle that she had brought as part of her medicine pouch. It became a smelly purple color and when it got to be a pasty thickness, she spread the goo on the bite, and then placed her hand over the medicine. She said a little prayer and looked upward. Everyone looked upward, and KwoNeShe's mother began singing a chant to the Great Spirit to save her baby.

Isobel took the scrap of cloth from Katherine's dress and dipped it in the water then wrapped tied the baby's arm to make sure the wound stayed clean to give the medicine a chance to heal the arm and draw the poison out of the wound.

All they could do now was sit and wait.

Chapter 19- The Gift

The day turned into evening and the evening drifted into full night. The women who helped Isobel with the baby boy were needed back with their families. Isobel and KwoNoShe's mother stayed with the child.

"Katherine, please go tell your father where I am and what I am doing. You will have to fix dinner this evening. You may come back, if you like. I am staying here with the baby. He may need more of the poultice. Thank you Katherine."

Isobel continued the treatment of the child. His mother stayed close by, watching every move Isobel made.

She moved closer, took Isobel's hand gently in hers and held it to her heart. She smiled at Isobel and did not need to say anything. Isobel knew what she was doing. The boy's mother was grateful for the medicine and the care Isobel was giving to her child. She knew that she did not have to worry about her son, especially since Isobel was from the fort. KwoNeShe's mother had no expectations from Isobel. She just somehow knew the medicine Isobel was treating her baby with was working. They both sat and patiently waited.

Isobel began to yawn and nod off. KwoNeShe's mother asked Isobel her name.

Isobel held her hand to her chest and said "I-so-bel." KwoNeShe's mother said "Cikala Heton," meaning Little Antelope.

Cikala Heton motioned to the blanket that lay on the floor of the tipi. She directed Isobel to the blanket and gently covered her in blankets. Isobel fell fast asleep.

Little Antelope continued the watch over here child and quietly continued her prayer song of healing to the Great Spirit.

The hours slowly ticked by. Wispy clouds traveled overhead and sunrise gave a beautiful crimson glow to the start of the new day.

The baby was beginning to stir, and a tiny moan was heard. Isobel arose with a start, and Cikala Heton went quickly to her child's side.

Isobel carefully unwrapped the boy's arm to see how the medicine was working.

The bandage was spotted with the baby's blood,

but with a strange yellowish color. It had worked!

The poultice had drawn the snake's poison out of the child. The baby was going to live. He would need more attention for a few days, so Isobel made another paste of the anti venom and treated the boy's arm with more of the pasty goo.

She showed Cikala Heton how to put it on the arm and told her daughter to tell her mother when to put more on the bite. Isobel picked up the boy and cradled him in his blanket then handed him to Cikala Heton.

His mother was sobbing with happiness to have her baby boy in full life once again. The smile she smiled at Isobel was enough. Isobel gave Cikala Heton a hug and then left the tipi.

Isobel knew the boy was much better and would be fine in his mother's care.

She had to get back to her own family and take care of them. She was sure they were wondering what happened.

Jacob was outside the wagon with Jakie. They were greasing the wagon wheels with bacon fat and mending any broken spokes that might have begun to shrink from going through the rivers.

Jacob walked over to his wife and smiled, "Katherine told me what you were doing. I am proud of you, Isobel. Is the boy all right?"

Isobel told them of the events of the previous night and what it was that helped the boy survive the deadly snakebite. She excused herself and went

to get some more rest in the wagon.

"You children have a wonderful mother. Do you know that?" Jacob said.

They were all feeling pride for their mother. She was truly a medicine woman. Afternoon drew near. Isobel awoke from her well-deserved nap and looked outside the wagon to see what time of day it was.

There she saw Cikala Heton and her entire family sitting patiently, waiting for Isobel to come out of the wagon. Isobel brushed herself off and climbed down off the wagon. Cikala Heton got up and went to Isobel. Cikala Heton had her baby wrapped in the blanket and showed Isobel how well he was doing. The baby was smiling, and his eyes were bright with color and playing with his rattle. Isobel could not help smile when she saw the child's progress.

Cikala Heton said a few words and KwoNeShe translated as best she could.

My mother and father have brought a gift for you.

It is to thank you for saving our little one. My father is our Chief. You have brought great joy to our clan by saving this life in our family.

KwoNeShe's Father was wearing a large, ceremonial white buffalo robe. He took it from his back and placed it over Isobel's back. It was so heavy it almost brought Isobel to the ground. The children helped her with the robe to keep their mother from falling over.

KwoNeShe said, "This buffalo robe is a gift for

the medicine woman. She will always be part of our family. Your family will be safe from all harm and all Omaha will know from where you received this robe and how you came by it."

Jacob watched from a distance to see the great honor Isobel was given. He just beamed. Mr. Biggs was standing next to him, "This is very special you know. They don't give a robe like that to anyone. You can believe this Jacob, we will need it where we are going.

The Pioneer Journey

Going West
Across the Great Divide

Book Two

Chapter 20- To the Rockies

A new sunrise warmed the anxious wagon party. Rubbing of eyes and stretching to the sky accompanied with the sounds of yawning were heard throughout the camp. The sounds of men clearing their throats and the clattering of pots and pans welcomed the new morning. The women began the chore of cooking the breakfasts for each of the families. The men, and everyone else who could, tended the chores of checking the wagons and checking the supplies that were left, and needed to get stocked for the next trail.

Jakie junior helped his father, Katherine and Katey cleaned up Emily and got her ready, and their mother Isobel managed to do everything else. She was talented and able that way.

Chapter 20- To the Rockies

Mr. Biggs, called everyone to the daily train meeting and began to let them all know where they were about to travel. "Only a few days left in our stay here at Fort Kearney, folks. Then, we will be on our way to the halfway point at Fort Laramie in the west. Over these times, you make sure you have all your provisions taken care of and your wagons are trail ready. If any of the beasts are sickly leave them here. You can pick up new animals at Laramie. The road is pretty even and straight so you won't need full teams right away," Mr. Biggs told the meeting of families.

"What we will be doing when we get to Fort Laramie, is preparing for the worst. We are going to double our supplies, making sure the teams are well and rested. We have quite a climb ahead of us. We will be going through one of the lower passes, but it is still pretty high. Five thousand feet. We will be scraping the sky up there. We are going to take it slowly just a few miles a day. Hopefully, the weather will stay with us and the air won't get too thin. It gets hard to breathe in some parts up in the mountains. The animals will have just as hard a time breathing as we will. So remember, if the teams slow down we stop right there, so they can rest. I will keep notice of a water supply and where good pasture land is on the trail ahead. I want to try to stay at those places for the nights. Any questions? The party of pioneers was partly excited and partly real cautious.

The Rocky Mountains are the highest stretch of land in the entire United States. No one had ever seen anything like them before, but they were about to.

Chapter 20- To the Rockies

In the next week they would see the beginnings of one of the highest mountain ranges on the continent of North America.

The one thing the Summers wagon party had in their favor, was the pass they were about to go through, had been traveled by thousands of wagons before, and many more would follow. They had faith in Mr. Biggs that he knew what and where to take the wagons and how to get them to their destination safely, barring any difficultieAll the wagon trains became a

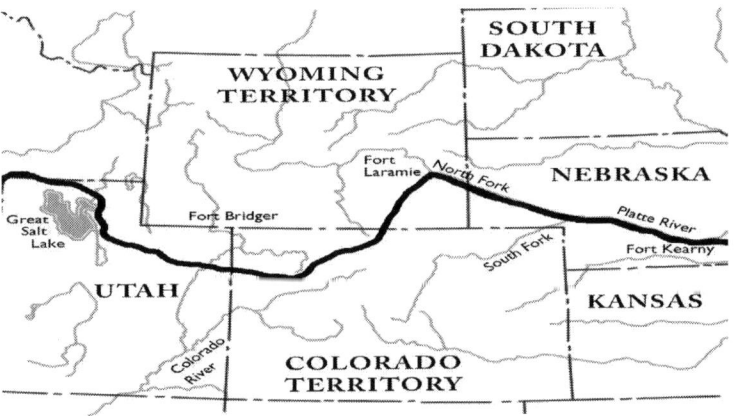

buzz with activity. The moos and whinnies of teams being led to new feeding pastures, and the clanking of pots and pans being cleaned and readied for the evening meals, along with the grunting of men and the chatting of the women echoed throughout the trail camp. Teams were being unhitched, wheels were being greased. Cooking fires were being assembled. Everyone was preparing for the evening.

Everyone was doing something to make sure the well being of their wagon party was taken care of. It was a sight to behold. Every hour was energized all evening long.

The cool of the evening came and everyone was settling down for the supper of what might be the last meal of fresh meat and vegetables they would eat for some time.

After supper time was over and done, the dinner chores were taken care of and everyone gathered together as if having a great town dance.

The musicians all played what they brought with them. Their guitars, banjos, fiddles, concertina filled the air with joyful melodies and dance tunes. Mrs. Smithers, a missionary lady, even played her small pump organ from the back of her wagon, to, as she said, give some convenient balance to the nights activities.

Everyone danced, sang, and had one very good time. Even the soldiers that had come celebrated with the pioneers. The soldiers appreciated the folks. Being alone way out on the territorial prairie was often lonely and sometimes known to drive a man out of his mind.

The lack of civilization and the constant boredom of the same thing day in and day out would get to you if you were not of a strong mind. The duties were the same no matter what day it was, or what time it was. If you were a soldier you did them over and over. It did not matter if you were in blistering hot sun or freezing and wind blown snow. You did what was needed because you had to survive. It became so tedious, many times,

Chapter 20 - To the Rockies

you could not even tell what day of the week it was or if it was a holiday like Christmas or what have you.

The parties these pioneer wagon trains celebrated were a welcomed event in the lives of these military men, even if it was only for a few hours. It made their lives a little more bearable out in the middle of nowhere.

Yes indeed, they truly enjoyed themselves.

Chapter 21- Gritting Teeth

All the wagons that had spelled for a time at Fort Kearney were now on the trail to Fort Laramie. Great long lines of covered wagons, buckboards, carts, and whatever the people had, rolled along the deep furrowed trail to the famous Fort Laramie in the Colorado and Wyoming territory.

The prairie was so wide it allowed for these long single filed streams of humanity to continue on the journey westward. The multiple rows of wagons rolled over the prairie like a parade going down a city street. In some trains there as many as 250 wagons filled with the hopes and dreams of every family who drew a breath. Some wagons were more rickety than others, nothing special in the way any of them looked. They had after all, been through some very treacherous trails.

Chapter 21- Gritting Teeth

Many of them appeared as if they would simply fall apart if they went any farther. A wheel might go off, or a harness might just turn to dust. The canvas covers on a great deal of them were no longer there, and those that survived only had a few more days left in them. They had been torn to tatters, shredded into rags that barely gave any shade or privacy at all. It was not easy to keep shaded and cool with out the much needed wagon covers.

The travelers did the best they could with the supplies and moneys they had left. Some left with all they had, and that was not enough. They became dependent on the generosity of others in their trains, by either trading labor for supply or helping on hunts for game on the prairies. Much of the time, folks were just staying behind to homestead when their stakes ran out. Where they stopped was where they made their new home. It was not a smooth and easy decision to make. Most made their new homesteads from sod and clay from the ground. That meant digging. A lot of digging and many days of being in the hot sun, before any help or hope would arrive.

It was only a three days ride to Fort Laramie, but it seemed like it would take forever. In some of the other wagon trains we saw along the trail, wheels fell off, folks took sick, and wagons broke down. These were all the things Mr. Biggs told us to be ready for before we hit the trail back at Fort Kearney. He was right.

But all our wagons were doing just fine. No one was sick and we were in good spirits. It did not matter that some of our wagons were not in the best of shape, we were all still together. Even the Hawkins family wagon was doing better.

Since after the big storm we weathered through, all the men pitched in and helped make sure the Hawkins

Chapter 21- Gritting Teeth

wagon would make it, at least to Ft. Laramie.

The trail went alongside the south bank of the Platte River. Soon it was to change course in three different directions. Some folks took the south fork trail. Others went northerly to Oregon. Our train headed straight to California.

The south fork, we were told, was the hardest. It went through hostile Indian territories and most of time the pioneers never made it to their destinations. The weather usually killed them. They were headed for high deserts and summer was not over. It was to be hotter than a stoked wood stove. Either the animals would die due to lack of water or the people would get heated and go desert mad. If their wagon masters knew the trails south, they might stand a chance. Many of them were on their own without any clue of direction or knowledge of what to expect. The odds were against them.

The three days passed quick as a wink. Fort Laramie in the distance was as big as any city they had ever seen in Minnesota. The buildings counted over one hundred and fifty, not including the tents that were outside the fort.

Fort Laramie did not have any walls like Kearney did, so it was easy to count and see everything.

It was so spread out; it was hard to tell where it began and where it ended. It also had an Indian camp on the outskirts, much bigger than the camp at Ft. Kearney.

There were horses. Hundreds of horses. Grazing in the fields next to the six stable buildings. They had never seen so many horses in one place before, except maybe when they went to town on a holiday.

"Mama, are we going to stay here as long as we did at Fort Kearney?" Katherine asked.

"You should ask your Father. He will know,"

Isobel answered.

Katey looked outward into the distance. Katherine and Jakie noticed and he gently poked her arm."

"What are you staring at?" Jakie asked.

Katey just pointed to the horizon.

"You see em?"

"See what?" Katherine asked.

"I can just see them. They are a far piece off yet, but they are there. Sitting straight up as big as you please. They go from here to there without saying a word, but they sure enough let you know they are there.

They must be the biggest things on earth," Katey said.

Katey was gazing at the Rocky Mountains. She saw the beginnings of the foothills, but even those were

Chapter 21- Gritting Teeth

plenty big. "Aren't they the most beautiful things you ever saw?" Katey asked.

"When we get closer, they are going to seem impossible. They get higher and even higher when you get inside them. They just keep growing until they are so close to the clouds, that birds have to duck down so they don't hit their heads on the sky."

Katey was mesmerized by the grandeur of this great natural dividing line.

"Katey, how do you know about these mountains? You sound like you been there before," Jakie asked.   "Books! You remember books. I think you said you read one once didn't you?" Katey smartly answered. Katherine giggled at Jakie for being such a smart aleck. "That's telling him, Katey."

Jakie scrunched up his face and stuck out his lower lip and pouted with his arms crossed.

"Come on now , we have chores to do.," Katey reminded

Chapter 22- Halfway Home

Katherine, Katey, and Jakie got busy with their chores. Jacob arranged for the family to sleep in a barracks building that wasn't being used. The Fort Commander gave Mr. Biggs permission for the wagon party to gather whatever they needed to get back on the trail. Commander Collins even assigned a special attaché for the people of the train.

"If you would be so kind, you folks are to let Sergeant Riddle know what you need and he will be sure to get it for you."

The Commander turned and tipped his hat to Isobel Summers and continued with his duties of the fort.

"Mama, what do you think he meant? Did he really say we could have whatever we need?" Katherine asked.

Chapter 22- Halfway Home

"I am sure he meant what he said. The fort is here to make sure all the folks in these parts are safe and provided for. This is the halfway point of the trail for many of us and the Commander wants to make double sure we all get safely to our destination.

Don't you children go asking for anything silly like candied licorice or gumdrops. We need to get only the supplies that will get us to California. You hear me? Now go on with your chores," Isobel said.

The children unloaded the wagon and set all their belongings on the covered porch of the barracks building. They brought their clothing and personal items inside. The ladies who lived at Fort Laramie with their soldier husbands greeted the ladies of the wagon train and invited them all to a social to be held for just the women of the fort.

"Jacob, I am going to that social at the fort dance hall.

I deserve some rest. Children, you do as your father says. Don't get into mischief." After the adventures on the trail, Isobel felt she needed to have a time for some simple talking and socializing amongst other ladies. They had teacakes and special fruit punch and tea drinks in very small teacups..

Jacob told the children, "We have to sort everything.

I mean everything. Little Jake – oh, excuse me young sir." Jacob said bowing and tipping his hat to his son. – "Jakie, you scoop out the flour from the barrel."

"Papa," Jakie whined. "I always have to do that. Can't one of the girls do it this time?"

"Jacob Summers Jr., you mind me at once, or no play time this evening, you hear?" Jacob took off his hat and

Going West/ Across The Great Divide

Chapter 22- Halfway Home

swatted Jakie's backside to get him on his way.

"Katey, you and Katherine gather all the clothes and get to washing."

The girls loaded the clothes into pillowcases and brought the whole load to the washing trough. There they met other young ladies and some older women who where doing their monthly laundry. It was funny how everyone had pretty much the very same items to wash. There were uniforms, undergarments, lots of socks to be darned, overcoats and gloves, and blankets to be washed. There were lots of blankets. Most were dark blue woolens and needed to be carefully washed so they would not shrink and the colors would not run, though they did anyway. There was nothing like a short-sheeted blanket that just won't cover you on a cold night. Brrrrrrr.

The heat of the day was soon interrupted by a cold wind rushing over the plains from the foothills of the Rocky Mountains. Everyone went from sweating in the hot sun and blowing dust, to almost freezing in the blink of an eye.

"What do we do with the clothes? Papa will be upset at us if they are left out to get dusty again, especially since we just washed them all," Katherine said.

"We still need to hang them to dry, but with this wind and dust flying around, it will be just about impossible to get them all dried and neat."

Katey suggested, "What don't we get some rope and hang them in the back of the barracks building.

There is hardly any wind and they won't get as dusty."

The girls gathered all the still soaking wet clothes and rung them out as best they could. They brought them

Going West/ Across The Great Divide

to the back of their lodgings. You could tell where they went by the trail of water streaming on the ground like a snail trail marking a path.

The girls asked Jakie to find some rope and he was more than willing to go find some, anything to get away from the flour barrel and looking for flour maggots.

Jakie brought the rope around to the back of the barracks and took one end of it, while the girls took the other.

"Now where to tie it up?" Katherine said. "Jakie, you take your end and tie it to that tree over there.

I will tie it off over here on this other tree."

Jakie tied his end onto the leftovers of a small oak tree and called out, "it's tied on."

Katherine and Katey took the other end and found the perfect spot to tie the rope. They found a branch about the same height as Jakie's tree, but high enough off the ground so the clothes would not touch dirt and low enough so they could hang the laundry. There was one problem. On the branch Katherine chose, was an almost invisible hive of honeybees. The girls saw a few bees but thought nothing of them. They were familiar with honey bees. Katherine always helped her father with them back on the farm, so she figured it would be all right to be so close.

She found an old stump nearby large enough for her to stand on. From there, she could throw the rope over and tie it down. Katherine gathered the rope in one hand and did her best to toss it over the intended limb, but she missed.

She coiled up the rope again, threw it, and missed

Chapter 22- Halfway Home

again, only this time the rope hit the bee hive, and what seemed to be thousands of bees, and they all suddenly came after them.

Unfortunately, there was something very attractive about the laundry soap they used. The bees liked it more than the two girls cared to know. They dropped the freshly washed clothes and began swatting in circles, faster and faster. There was only one thing to do.

The girls yelled out, "RUN!"

Chapter 23- Tending the Stings

The girls were in a soup this time. The bees swarmed after the two scalawags as if they had the secret to all the nectar in the world.

The girls could not run fast enough. They swatted and slapped at the bees and got stung again and again.

"Ouch! Ye-ow!" They screamed as they ran all over the back of the barracks yard. Jakie began to laugh, but thought he should help his sister and her friend before they really got hurt.

"Run to the pig pen and jump in the mud! The bees won't get you there," Jakie called out.

Round and round they ran, trying to get away from the swarm.

Chapter 23 - Tending the Stings

Jakie ran to tell his Mama at the Ladies social.

"Sorry ladies, but… Mama, come quick! We hit a beehive and…"

Isobel quickly ran out the door with a few of the other women right behind her.

"Where are they, Jakie?"

"Behind the barracks building," he said, pointing.

Jakie ran ahead of the ladies to show them the way. Isobel and another woman snatched up a few wet blankets from the clotheslines. They found Katherine and Katey running for their lives. The ladies instantly covered the two victims with the blankets and brought them to the ground. The ladies suffered a few stings themselves, but soon the bees retreated and the girls were safe and even more sorry.

"What happened? Where did they all come from?" Isobel asked.

Katherine was sniffling and moaning as she whined, feeling every sharp tiny barb as she answered.

"Oh, I was trying to be clever and dry the clothes after washing. We were gong to tie a rope to the tree and I hit a beehive with the rope we were gonna use to hang the laundry. I thought the clothes would be okay if they were drying in back of the barracks where there was no wind, until the bees started after us. I'm sorry Mama."

"I don't think you'll be doing that again any time soon. No need to be sorry, but you did give us all a fright.

Let's get you both to the infirmary and take care of

Chapter 23 - Tending the Stings

those stings, but first we need to get you cleaned up.

You two smell like a barnyard." Isobel said turning away.

The two girls stumbled to their feet and painfully walked to the water trough slowly and the ladies cleaned up the two adventurers as carefully as they could.

The cold water helped ease the pain of the stings a little. Then to the fort hospital where they could get proper medical care and rest. Sopping wet and in pain, they saw the place they would call home for at least a week.

After carefully laying down, the Doctor began to take each stinger out one by one. Some of them did not come out as easily as others. With each pluck of a stinger, the girls let out an ouch and a whimper, and with each whimper a tear fell down their cheeks. It felt like hundreds of stingers, but really it was only an about a dozen.

But with each stinging, pain filled, tiny barb, came a blistering reminder of how foolish they had been.

Jacob found out about the commotion and went to see how the girls were doing. He stood at the entrance to the hospital and watched the two cringe and wince with every yank of every tiny stinger.

Katherine looked up and did not know what was going to be worse; her father's punishment for not getting the clothes cleaned or suffering through the bee stings as they healed.

Jacob came in and sat down in between them.

"You two had quite and adventure today.

Let me ask you something. Will you do as I ask

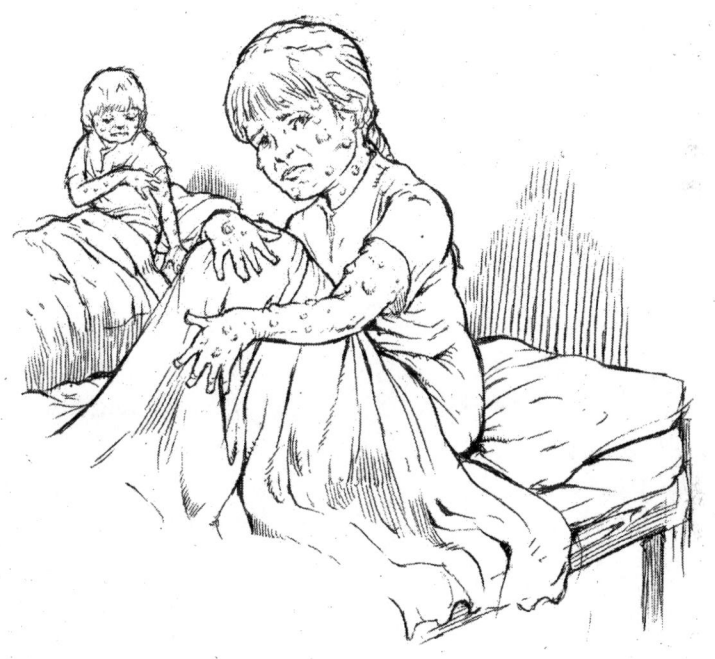

Chapter 23 - Tending the Stings

next time and not try to be clever, just do the best you can?"

Katherine's and Katey's faces were swollen with bee sting lumps, their arms were covered with bumps and red crimson welts. They both shook their heads yes.

"Doctor, how long before these two can get back to their mischievous selves?" Jacob asked.

"I would give them three to four days. That should be just enough time for the calamine and lavender oil to heal the stings. They are going to need a lot of it, so I expect they will be spending most of their time in here. They won't be dawdling about. There is plenty to do in here. I want to keep an eye on them for a few days anyway. Some of the stings are serious. They will need extra attention."

The girls looked at each other and sighed. They knew they had caused a ruckus and they doubly knew they had upset the entire fort by not being careful. Mostly, they felt very foolish.

"You see what you made us get into?" Katey said.

"What do you mean, I made us get into? You were in this, too. You held up the rope on the other end," Katherine argued.

"All right, you two, you have made enough problems for this fort. You rest and you behave, or I'll give you a duty in this hospital that no one likes, cleaning spittoons. You settle in, lie back, and be quiet!" the Doctor said.

The Doctor made sure they were not going to be a

disturbance to any of the patients who really needed his help.

The girls did as they were told. They lay back in their beds and slowly crossed their arms in disgust. They hoped the calamine would begin to work soon.

All you could hear with every movement was a quiet foolish felt, whimper, and a very meaningful "Ow!"

Chapter 23 - Tending the Stings

Chapter 24-
The Ascent

The week went by so fast, you could almost say it was a blink in time. That is what Mrs. Hawkins told Mama when they were packing up their wagons with new supplies – new flour, new water barrels, new bolts of cloth, even new hard tack, though no one knew hard tack could ever get old.

This was the government's way, according to Commander Collins, of making absolutely sure, well, almost absolutely sure, that all the immigrants crossing had a better chance of getting across the great divide and to where they were headed.

The Rockies were treacherous in places and could be filled with danger along the trail. He also said that there

Chapter 24- The Ascent

are many new towns sprouting up. Silver City was one of the newest and we should try to get there within the week, before the thunder and lightning storms came.

Mr. Biggs knew the way and was going to get us there, safe and sound.

But for us, we were still pink from a coating of Calamine covering our bee stings. It would not have been so bad if we didn't have stings on our faces. We looked as if we had an attack of small painful rubber balls stuck to our skin. The welts were getting smaller, but the pain wasn't. We were a sight. If we wore our long sleeves, the sun made us perspire and then the salt from our sweat would run down our arms and get into the stings and make them hurt all the more.

As it was, Mama made us cover our faces with handkerchiefs to protect our skin from the sun. No matter what we did, it was going to hurt. It was safe to say we learned to be very careful in whatever we did from then on.

We did the best we could to help Mama and Papa and Jakie load up, but our efforts were not much doings.

We could not wait to be rid of these hurtful lessons and get back to being able to do chores and play like we used to. We didn't know how long a time that sounded like until after we said it.

Sunset again, and the darkness of night came only to wake us again in the morning light. All the wagons with axles greased and new supplies loaded, were ready to go again.

"How many times do we do this, Mama?" Jakie asked.

"As many as it takes to get there, my boy. As many as it takes," Papa answered back.

Jacob was tending the oxen and double rigging the leathers and harnesses. He was making sure the rigging would stay together while the team was pulling the fully loaded wagon up the steep trails.

Commander Collins came out to say his goodbyes and wish us all a safe journey. He told us and a few of the other wagon parties that we would be escorted by a small patrol of soldiers to help us get through an area known for hostiles. There was an air of relief after he told us.

"Papa, what are hostiles?" Jakie asked

"I am sorry to say that many times, some of the people on this trail and Indians have not gotten along. Many times, the Indians were taken advantage of and much of their lands was taken by force by others who could take profit from the Indians lands. I reckon you might say the Indians were trying to defend what they have left. It would be much like you would do if someone tried to take your favorite hat or a your dog Sam. We have nothing to be worried about here. Your mama tended to that. Remember the Buffalo Robe Cikala Heton and the Chief gave her for saving their little one?"

Jakie nodded his head yes. He understood

Chapter 24- The Ascent

what his Father told him and took it to heart.

"Papa do you think we will have any trouble?"

"You know, son, trouble comes where you look for it. No, I don't think we will find any. You go and finish helping your mother. Your sister, Emily, is not doing well and she will need tending for a while.

Why don't you make double sure she has a good bed in the wagon. Fix up the quilt your grandmother made her. Use it for a mattress and put it on the side where the water barrels are. They will help keep her cool in this weather. I need you to help your mother in whatever way she needs. All right? Oh, and don't run off like you did before."

Jakie stopped and realized his Father knew what happened back at Fort Kearney. He turned and smiled, then went and did exactly as he was told.

Mr. Biggs checked on every wagon in the train and wished us all well. He rode back to the head of the wagon train and called out "Hey, Yooooooo!"

It was exciting. We were about to go into hostile territory, cross the highest mountains we had ever seen, and be halfway to California. Our metal was soon to be tested.

None of us expected what was to happen on the trail up ahead.

Chapter 25-
Tragedy on the Trail

On the trail out of Fort Laramie, there must have been a thousand wagons, carts and buggies of some sort or another. Each person on each of those conveyances had a wish, a dream, one great goal and desire to get to that special new place in their lives to make things better for themselves and their families. Whether it be to start up a new business, or to strike it rich in the California gold fields, or even to be able to find a stretch of land and farm it, they all had one wonderful yearning.

The folks who made it this far were encouraged by vision of the majestic Rocky Mountains. The mountains helped them realize this was the halfway point. The point of no turning back

Chapter 25- Tragedy on the Trail

was up ahead and it was either continue on or stay put now and homestead right where they stood. Some folks went home. Fear will do that to you if you don't have the spirit to persevere.

From a distance, you might say, that at the entrance where the wagons entered up into the foothills, it appeared as if the hillside was eatin' the long snake-like trail of pioneers. You only saw so far and they disappeared into the mountainside. Each had that side to side wobble navigating each bump and hole.

Each rock that stuck out of the ground made the ride more jarring. It was almost like being shaken out of your bones, and jerked about – much like the feeling you feel when you were trying to break a green filly. Each wagon was tossed about like a clipper ship on the high seas. The wagon ruts on the trail were so deep in places that the wagons bottoms scraped the ground as they passed over. When this happened, many times the men would have to stop to help lift and push the wagon up and out of the hole to get it on the way once more. It happened so often in places the contents of the wagons had to be taken out to make it easier for the men to lift the wagon and move it forward.

Mr. Biggs, as he always had done, rode up ahead to scout how the trail conditions were and he came back with a report.

"We have a climb on the ridge up a piece. It's not bad, but we need to be careful and all of us need to be sure that we walk up and only the wagons and supplies are teamed up. No wagon riders on this trail. It will make the journey a little quicker and easier on the teams. We are going to be in these Rockies for a fair time and we need to take care all the way."

All the wagons stopped. Everyone got out of their wagons and began to walk. Some who had an extra horse or mule gave saddle to a few of those who were unstable in stride or step, or who were too feeble to walk by themselves. Many of the folks who had joined the wagon train a ways back were older and were not going to make it up the ridge trail by walking. It wasn't a hard climb, but they did have run-ins with more of those deep narrow wagon ruts. And a couple of times, folks had to have help to get their feet unstuck.

A few hours ticked by and the wagon train traveled smoothly on the California Road for a time, no deep ruts, no stopping to push a wagon. They even reached the top of the ridge, making things easier for the elders of the party to ride once more in their wagons in a more comfortable setting.

More and more trail passed underneath the wagons as the journey progressed. Mr. Biggs called out to rest in the clearing just ahead. There is water there and fresh grass for the animals.

An air of excitement exploded in the wagon train. People started whooping and hollering and snapping the whips to get the teams to move faster.

But, just as the folks were starting to celebrate, in a

Chapter 25 - Tragedy on the Trail

powerful way, Mother Nature let her presence known.

The sound of moving earth and rocks came from above on the left side of the wagon line. An avalanche slide like no one had ever seen, threw rocks and large boulders down on the wagons like a rain of brimstone. Stones and boulders of all sizes were raining down and coming like they were being thrown. The wagons weren't moving fast enough.

The Samuelson wagon was doomed. It was struck again and again and again. It was being pelted with a storm of gravel and large stones. One rock took the cover off the wagon and shredded it right off the frame. Most of the Samuelson family ran for shelter some steps away from their wagon. Thinking that it would be safe where they were taking cover, a large rock came down on Mr. Samuelson's arm and broke it. Just then a boulder hit a back wheel of their wagon and shattered it breaking the rear axle clean in two. The wagon collapsed to the ground.

Mr . Samuelson stood counting his family, very afraid he saw that his beloved wife Mary was not with them. With a look of horror he said.

"She's under the wagon!" Still looking to see if everyone was there with him he said, "Sarah, where's Sarah?"

Then, as fast as it started, the rock slide gently came to a stop. Citizens of the party scrambled to help lift the Samuelson's wagon. Heave ho! Heave ho! Everyone helped – men and women alike, even children who could lend a strong back – everyone pitched in.

Chapter 25 - Tragedy on the Trail

This was a matter of life and death. Men lifted the wagon and others helped comfort members of the Samuelson family.

All except for one.

Mrs. Samuelson was covering her youngest when the wagon collapsed. The four year old was alive and a bit shook up, but her mother was gone. Mary had suffered a fatal blow to her neck, breaking it.

A sad quiet covered the train. All that was heard were tears and sobbing. Not only had Mr. Samuelson and his family lost their beloved mother and wife, everyone in the wagon train had lost a dear friend.

Chapter 26- Slower to Silver City

The members of the wagon train were quiet for the rest of the day. Mr. Samuelson stood there looking outward at the land they had worked so hard to get to. Four of his children stood along side. He held his fifth, Sarah, in his arms very closely.

Tears rolled down his face as he cried with a silent strength. He knew what had to be done now. There was no going to California. There was no meaning to the journey without Mary. He had been going to California with his whole family to get a better life for them all. He thought perhaps this had happened as a way of telling him that this place was supposed to be their new home.

His oldest son, Michael, asked if he was going to be alright. He told his father he would be right with him to help, just as Mary had told him to do every day of the trip. Mr. Samuelson took out his kerchief and blew the sniffles from his nose and wiped a tear from his eye. He was truly touched by his son's willingness to help.

Jacob placed his hand on Mr. Samuelson's shoulder, "Jeremiah, bring the children over here while the women prepare Mary for her rest."

"Jacob, I thank you all for helping Mary and us. I would not have known what to do, but I do know what needs to be done now. I reckon it's a way of telling us, for some reason, we are to stay right where we are. I can't leave Mary like this. We will homestead here. I'll build my farm here with my children. It is a pretty place. Mary always liked pretty places. She will like it here."

Jeremiah began to ramble about when he spoke.

"Come over here and sit for a spell my friend," Jacob said. "You need some rest."

While Mary was being prepared for her burial, Jeremiah Samuelson noticed that one of his team was down on the ground and the other was injured. The oxen team had been hurt. One had a broken leg and the other had long scratches and deep cuts from falling and tumbling rocks.

"There is no possible way we can go any further now that the team is down. I'll have to shoot one and hope the other survives. We need to have at least one of the oxen to drag the plow and logs for the cabin we'll need. Michael, you stay here with your brothers and sisters. I have things to do," Jeremiah said.

The ladies of the wagon train dressed Mary Samuelson in her best dress and decked her out in best Sunday go to meetins. They wanted her to look good so she could meet her maker with respect and perhaps even a little style.

One of the men made a quick coffin for her out of some extra building boards he brought to build his new store that he hoped to have in California. The women laid Mary inside the pine square box, and then Isobel went to tell Mr. Biggs everything was ready.

From the Samuelson's wagon there was a sudden BOOM. Jeremiah Samuelson had shot the ox that had the broken his leg.

"Here, you all take this animal and use it for tonight's supper. Mary would say there is no sense in being wasteful."

With two horses and a rope rigging, the large ox was dragged off for butchering for the supper meal. Everyone would be eating hearty that night.

Mr. Biggs brought all his strength forward so he could apologize to Mr. Samuelson. Gridley walked over to him and shook his hand and hung his head in shame.

"This is the first time there has ever been a death on any of my wagon trains. I am so sorry What are your plans now?"

Jeremiah explained to Biggs how this was a perfect place for Mary to be, and how the children would earn up to her expectations as people right here. They would grow up just fine in this spot.

This way their Mother could watch over them close by.

A few men helped in the digging of the grave and it wasn't long after they were finished with a perfectly shaped grave-site of fresh earth that Mary Samuelson's coffin was carried to her final resting place. Everyone gather together and stood around Mrs. Samuelson's grave. Heads were hung. Jeremiah held his children close he held the hand of the youngest one. Tears flowed from everyone, including the men.

Pastor Carter said some kind words for Mary, even though he did know her well. He did the say the Lord's Prayer and tried his best to deliver some words of encouragement for Mr. Samuelson and his family, but the words seemed to land flat in the dirt before our feet.

Mary Samuelson's death, no matter how accidental, placed a clouded dark mist over our heads. Our souls seemed to shrink deeply into our hearts for protection. None of us knew what to expect of the remaining journey, and now even Mr. Biggs' confidence seemed to wane.

Later that night, in the midst of supper, Jeremiah called out for everyone to come together. '

"Everyone, I thank you for all you have done for me

and mine today. Your friendship means much more now than ever. But now I feel Mary has told me to stay here and raise my family in this spot. I know it is not California and I know it's a fair piece off from Silver City, but we will make it. Our journey has ended here in these foothills. Mary would have said this – if any of you pass this way again, stop in for a warm bed and a rest. I extend that invitation to you all right now. It will be rough for a time but that's okay. We have done once before, and we can do it again."

Mr. Hawkins piped up and suggested, "Mr. Biggs, how about we all pitch in and go one more step for Jeremiah and the children? Winter's not far off and building a cabin by himself will be difficult with his broken arm and all. His children and his provisions won't hold through the cold months, especially in these mountains. Why don't we stay and help build his new home? We all have extra that we can give them. It will take no time at all with all of us!"

A resounding cheer went out!

Michael Samuelson looked into his father's eyes, tugged on his father's coattail and smiled.

Jeremiah did not have the words.

Chapter 27- Onward

The settlers of the Summer's wagon party stayed and helped the Samuelson family for two weeks to help them homestead. A cabin was built out of trees from the nearby forest, firewood was cut, and a corral was constructed for the oxen plus one extra that was given to the family from the Hawkins folks. Even bed frames for the family and a wood stove that the Hawkins had spare was put into place, and food to last them all through the cold months of the wintertime was placed inside the cabin and into the new pantry cupboard that some of the men who knew carpentry built.

Mary Samuelson was buried on what was now the family plot near a tall and shady pine tree.

Mrs. Samuelson's grave site was not big by any means, just big enough to hold her, with some spaces for her family members should they ever have need.

"I will build a fence to keep the large critters out," Jeremiah said. Mary's grave marker was a finely carved piece of woodwork made from a fallen nearby tree.

"Jeremiah, I can't give you this plow, but I will hitch it and furrow out the field for you. Perhaps you can get some of the winter feeds and crops spread before the first snap hits."

Samuel Hawkins rigged the plow he brought with him and began to plow out the field. It was a big area, a couple of acres. There was just enough to get started with planting some crops that would grow before winter came.

Michael Samuelson stood by his mother's grave.

"Mama, I will take care of Papa and the family. You don't need to worry. I know you are watching over us. You just rest now. It sure is pretty here. Papa said you would like it here because of that."

Michael's eyes began to well up with tears as he spoke with his mother. It was hard to realize that his years as a boy had suddenly ended. He was now a young man. He was determined to make his father and mother proud of the way he cared for the family.

A few more days went by. Mr. Biggs made double sure this time that everyone was ready to go safely and securely. It was his wish that nothing like this ever happened again.

Now, with everything settled and the Samuelson family in their new home, it was time for the rest of the families to be on the way again. They all said their goodbyes and shook hands, and got started.

The next stop would be a very welcomed Silver City. A city of about one thousand folks, which was a good size for these parts.

Silver City was only three days away and they needed to get there to replenish supplies. There was still a long way to go before they were out of the Rockies and into the Great Salt Lake Basin. The trails were worn, but safe. The route they had to take was not an easy one. It was the beginning of desert and a salty one at that. Many had traveled it before, but that nagging feeling of uneasiness Mr. Biggs carried with him now would ride with him for the rest of the journey.

Jeremiah Samuelson stood with his children at the front porch of the new cabin and homestead that was so kindly built by the family he would never see again.

The Samuelson family waved goodbye as the wagon train members waved back, starting on the road to Silver City.

"Mama?" Katherine asked. "Will Mr. Samuelson and his family be alright? They seem to have everything they might need. I was thinking that because this is a new territory for them and Mr. Samuelson must be a little unsure…"

Isobel said, "Young'un you are a kind-hearted soul. Jeremiah and his family will do fine. When they came to Garden City from the northern country in

Canadian territory, they knew no one and had nothing. They know people now and have everything they might need that we could give them. He has the children to help with the new cabin and Silver City isn't that far away, according to Mr. Biggs. It might be a bit rough to begin with, but they will be fine."

"Would you like us to bury you like Mary Samuelson was?" Jakie asked.

"Why, don't you be putting me in the ground too soon, boy!" Isobel exclaimed.

"No, I don't mean that. It was just so pretty there. I thought you might like to be in a pretty place," Jakie explained.

"Don't you worry about that, son. At least not now, for my sake," Isobel said.

The wagons trekked up the road to Silver City and stopped for a short rest. After all, they had built a farm, a cabin, and then continued on a long journey, all within a few days time and everyone was tired and then some.

Mr. Biggs, as was his way, came back to update everyone on the distance left to travel before they had a well-deserved night's sleep.

Many days had passed before them without a good night's rest with fears and troubles that made them all wonder if the trip to California was worth the churning in each of their stomachs. A death and attacks by bees. The problems encountered on the trail were sometimes too much to bear. Some figured Silver

City in the Colorado territory was going to be it for them. This would be where they would settle.

A few more hours and they would be to a real city. A place, they thought, that would have hot baths and maybe a place to buy some dry goods and material for new clothes. But then, just before they entered the city limits, town deputies stopped them.

"Sorry, folks, we can't let you in. The town has whooping cough. You have to take the long way around Silver City. Don't know how it came in. All we know is what we have been sent to do. That is make sure no one gets in or out until this passes.

There have been 20 deaths because of it.

We don't want you or your families catching it.

The wagon train stopped. Everyone was wondering. Jacob took his cap off and asked.

"Now what Mr. Biggs?" Jacob said scratching his head.

Chapter 28-
The Celebrity

"Silver City is filled with the whooping cough, Mr. Biggs. Where are we going to get fresh supplies?" Mr. Hawkins asked.

Mr. Biggs thought for a moment and scratched his chin.

"The next town is three days off. Do you all think you have enough to get there?" He called out.

"Arvada is a smaller town and the chances of them having the whooping cough are slim. I think we should try for it."

Everyone agreed except one of the members, Mr. Hamill. He decided he would ask one more time. He wanted to try to connive his way into Silver City and around the deputies.

"Sir, I had the whooping cough when I was young.

I cannot catch it again. I have business in Silver City and must attend my meeting. May I go through?" Mr. Hamill said quite deliberately.

The deputy, holding his shotgun at the ready, walked up to get a closer look at Mr. Hamill.

"What exact business do you have in Silver City, mister?"

"I am to meet a gentleman in your fair town to discuss some mining prospects. These are of great importance to me and to my colleagues back in Nebraska City. They are expecting me to wire them about a particular silver and copper mining operation to which they have invested. I must get into town." Mr. Hamill explained.

"You wait right here, mister."

The deputy walked back to his partner. They chatted for a short time and one of them pulled out a poster from his back pocket. He unfolded it and shared the contents. Mr. Hamill was wanted for swindle and attempted thievery. The deputy waved Mr. Biggs over to explain what was about to occur. From atop his horse, Mr. Biggs reached down to shake their hands turned and galloped up to Mr. Hamill.

"It was nice knowing you, Mr. Hamill. I am sure you will enjoy your stay in Silver City. They have a room waiting for you right next to the saloon."

The lawmen nodded their heads in agreement and waved Mr. Hamill and his wagon through.

After the wagon passed the guard post of the

deputies, one of them jumped aboard Hamill's wagon and took the lines.

"What is this? This is an outrage, sir. I am perfectly capable of piloting this wagon into town.

Hand me back those lines," Mr. Hamill demanded.

"You have nothing to worry about. We were told to let through anyone who had important business that could not wait, and to make sure they had the best room in Silver City. That is where I am taking you right now," the deputy said, knowing right well where Mr. Hamill was going to stay for a very long time.

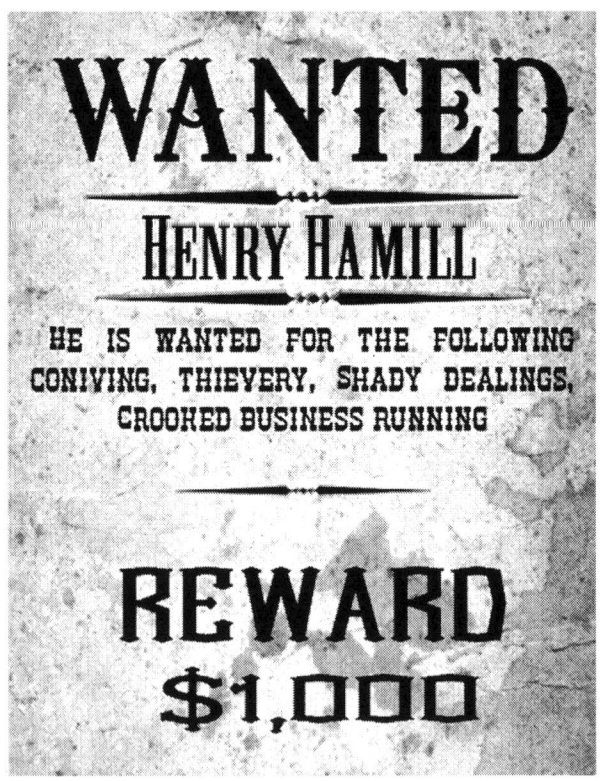

Mr. Biggs just waved to Mr. Hamill, wearing a big smile. Mr. Biggs was happy to see the scoundrel go. The train did not need to have anyone of that sort tagging along and making trouble for the rest of the folks.

"Mr. Biggs, why did that man get to go into Silver City and not the rest of us?" Mr. Hawkins asked.

"It turns out Mr. Hamill had a paper dispatched on him for being a scoundrel and a conniver. He is wanted in three territories and two reservation outposts. If those deputies had not taken him, Hamill would have tried to do his dirty deeds among us and he may have easily gotten himself hanged. So, I said goodbye to him and his ways and let the law handle it. Who knows, maybe the whooping cough will give an early retirement to Mr. Hamill."

Mr. Biggs finished his explanation and rode back to the front of the wagon train and with his familiar call to move on, "HEY YOOOOO."

The wagons started towards to the town of Arvada in the Colorado Territories. The wagon train had three days of smoother trails and one less problem to worry about. They were glad that Mr. Biggs said his goodbyes to the man who could have snake oiled his way into many pioneer purses and taken the train members for much of their hard earned futures.

Further down the trail, a small coughing was heard coming from the Summer's wagon.

Again the hacking raspy wheeze of coughing sounded, and it became louder and even more congested. Isobel yelled out to Jacob.

"Stop the wagon!"

She jumped into the back and found little Emily with a high fever. She was coughing as never before. The little girl was dripping with perspiration from the fever, almost turning a bright red from coughing so hard.

Jacob ran to Mr. Biggs and told him what was happening.

The wagons stopped once again and the news of Emily's sickness spread fast.

She had not been well ever since the family had left Garden City, Minnesota. It seemed like she had gotten over the croup and was fine, until now.

Jacob unloaded the large tub from the wagon and ladies from other wagons came to help.

"Jacob, we need a fire and we need to boil as much hot water as will fill the tub.

Emily has the whooping cough.

Katherine, you go tell Mr. Biggs to keep the other wagons moving up the trail. No sense in having any one else catching this. Tell him we will be along when we can up along the way.

Run! Hurry!"

Chapter 29-
The Long Watch

The Summers family had traveled so far without any major difficulties. They survived a deluge of rain and dust, lived in a cave for week, experienced winds that would knock down a stone house, and they lived through the sadness of friends when they lost a member of their family.

Jacob wondered before if he made the best decision in setting out for California. Nervously, he paced up and down what was now a pathway he carved into the dirt. Continuing to rub the back of his neck, his worry grew and grew. His only saving grace was the presence of his children and his beloved wife, Isobel.

Without them, he would have given it all up. No man was supposed to go through the heartache and troubles they all had just gone through.

Jakie sat next to a nearby oak tree, watching his father go through an agonizing time. What if the same thing that happened to Jeremiah's family, happens to us, Jacob thought. He still carried the nagging, horrible worry, about whether bringing the family to California, was the right choice.

"Papa, Emmy is going to be alright. Mama is very good at taking care of us. She won't let anything happen to Emily. Mama knows more about healing folks than anyone I know. She healed the Indian baby, didn't she?" Jakie said, trying to help his father feel better.

Jakie tried his best to reassure his father. It worried him to see his Papa act this way. Jakie knew that Emily was very sick. He remembered how his mother took care of him when he had the whooping cough. Jakie recalled the hard cough – the deep cough that rattled his chest so hard he thought it was going to explode and his lungs would jump out of his ribs. Jakie knew that Emily was not going to have an easy time of it. The fever that came with this form of consumption was always high until the ailment ran its course. Its favorite target always seemed to be small children. The overall population of the western territories had been depleted, at one point, by disease. This disease and other forms, from small pox and measles, to things like bad drinking water and cholera, were responsible for most of the deaths and severe sickness of the time. It overcame the older folks and the children.

Isobel called out, "Jacob, bring the water. Quickly Please! Jakie, Katherine help your father bring the buckets."

Katey stood watching and thinking about what Isobel did that helped to heal the Indian baby. She ran to get some of the herbs and flowers Isobel and Katherine told her about to make a poultice to apply to Emily. Katey ran back as fast as she could and jumped into the wagon, got the medicine pouch that Isobel kept with the mortar and pestle and began to grind the herbal concoction into the medicine that would help Emily.

When the poultice was ready she ran it back to Isobel and Emily.

"Isobel, here. This is for the baby," Katey said, handing over the paste.

"Child, you get back. You should not be here. You could catch the cough," Isobel cautioned. Katey started to go when Isobel interrupted her departure, "Katey, thank you dear. Now go."

Katey smiled at Isobel when she felt a tug on her dress. Jakie and Katherine were trying to get her to help them get the buffalo robe out of the wagon and bring it to their mother. Somehow, the children knew this special robe possessed special healing powers only to be used by Isobel, the medicine woman.

"Don't let it drag on the ground," Katherine said.

"It's so heavy," Jakie said.

"Come on, just a little further," Katey encouraged.

Jacob saw the children lugging the buffalo robe and went to help take up some slack and more of the weight.

"Where are you going with the beast's hide?" Jacob asked.

Katherine said, "The Chief said this robe was filled with special healing spirits for the medicine woman. He said mama was the medicine woman.

Maybe it will help mama make Emily well."

This was the first time Jacob heard any of the children express any concern for the success of their mother and for the well being of their little sister.

It was going to be a bumpy road ahead for the youngest of the Summers family. It would be several more days before daylight shone brightly once again for the hope-filled family. Emily had been a very sickly child from the day she was born. Now it appeared her journey was about to come to a congested halt on a trail in a territory where she appeared to be destined to live out the rest of her all to short life.

Jacob wrapped the baby in the robe and told Isobel to get some rest. Many of the women who stayed to help fell asleep having worked many hours alongside Isobel taking care of Emily.

Time was on Emily's side and the blessing of the Great Spirit that lived inside the special robe surrounded Emily's body as if providing guardian angels to help her get through this ordeal.

Jacob sat with Emily in his lap for much of the night, while he looked to the stars and asked for his little girl to be spared.

Chapter 30- A New Day

Isobel and the children awoke after a long night of worry and the sound of Emily coughing. Isobel had none to little sleep, so Jacob took over and stayed with Emily the entire night and did not budge from his little daughter's side.

Jakie, Katherine, and Katey, along with the women who stayed to help Isobel, were busy preparing more of the medicinal poultice for Emily.

Jacob rubbed the grit from his eyes and stretched out as high as his arms would let him then reached down to the ground to get the kinks out of his back.

"How is she this morning?" Isobel asked.

"She slept straight through the night. Just a few peeps from this little one," Jacob said.

He yawned with a mouth so wide you could jump down and come back up without fear of being swallowed.

Isobel lifted Emily from her father's arms, keeping her warm with a clean blanket. The buffalo robe was the saving grace for both Emmy and Jacob during that night.

The night air turned cold and the blanket's special healing gift kept both father and daughter free from any discomfort or intemperate weather conditions.

"Mama, is Emmy going to be alright? She hasn't felt well the entire time we have been gone from home. You think she is going to die?" Jakie asked.

"Young man, you watch your tongue. Little sister is going to be fine and I do not want to hear any more of that kind of talk. DO YOU HEAR ME?" Isobel scolded.

Jakie hung his head in shame and said, "I'm sorry."

Katherine gave Jakie a small shove for saying what he said.

"Hey! What was that for?" Jakie said.

Katherine continued to scold her brother.

"Sometimes, I declare, Jacob Summers Junior, you are such a nitwit. Mama and Papa are doing their very best to get Emily back to health and make her well again, then you come along and ask something so all fired stupid. What's is wrong with your head boy? If you weren't my brother, I think ...."

Katey spoke up, "Katherine, look, Emily is waking up and she isn't coughing!"

The children ran over to their little sister. Isobel was holding her and cradling her in the buffalo robe.

"Mama, the robe? Do you think it's the robe doing the healing? She's not coughing any more," Katherine asked.

Jacob answered his eldest daughter's question.

"There are more things unseen in heaven and on earth, and I believe the prayers and the healing gift your mama has, along with the robe, all gave us our Emily back."

Isobel said, "Jacob, no one I have ever known has ever gotten over the whooping cough in three days. She's not coughing and her fever is gone, touching Emily's forehead. I cannot take credit for healing this one. I wish I could. I would have given anything to get her back and keep her from going through this, but this is something more than I could have ever done."

"Mama does this mean we can still go to California?" Jakie asked.

"Yes, it does. You be aware young–un' Emily is not out of the dark yet. We need to watch her some more at least until tomorrow. Jacob, what do you think?" Isobel asked.

"If you think Emmy can travel, then we can head out first thing in the morning. Jakie, you know what to do. Go get the team. Girls, you get things straightened up and packed up. We'll get the chores done, Isobel. You just rest and take care of the little one.

Oh, and ladies, on behalf of my family and myself, I wish there was a way to thank you.

Words don't come to me at the moment."

For the first time in a very long time Jacob Summers was without anything to say. He very humbly took off his hat and held it to his chest and said a quiet thank you to all who helped his family stay a family.

The day drew on and the next morning arrived quick, and with it the clatter of pots and pans which woke the small band with the smells of breakfast and fresh coffee brewing over the campfire.

The wagon was ready to go. The team of oxen was fresh fed and watered and the skies were blue once more for the Summers family. Off they went, continuing along the trail in hopes they would be able to catch up with the rest of the train.

"What will we do if we cannot find the wagon train again, Papa?" Katherine asked.

"Well, I can try to find another train to join and go where they do, and just hope that they are going to California , or we can decide to find a piece of land and homestead it for our new home," Jacob said.

"Jacob Summers, we have come this far and I am not about to settle on some plot of land short of our new home. Don't you dare give up your dream!" Isobel chided.

"You are in some feisty mood, today Isobel. Remind me not get you upset at me for the rest of the journey," Jacob said, kidding. "Alright, let's get on. We have a long ways to go and a short time to catch the rest of the train."

"Daylight is in short order and we have lost three

days of trail time. But,who knows, we just have to keep our eyes forward and feet planted one step at a time. You can bet we will get to California right soon."

Chapter 31-
A Pleasant Surprise

The Summers family and three of the other families gathered up their grip and took to the trail once more. This time they switched directions and headed southward towards the Great Saddle. The Great Saddle was an easier transitional trail that made a way for earlier pioneers to travel over the backbone of the Rocky Mountains. It was a gradual assent and not so steep that the teams and wagons would suffer from the climb. It peaked at five thousand six hundred feet, and was the most beautiful stretch of land they ever saw. It was rolling hills and grasslands, with game that was there for the taking.

There was not a soul in sight for days. The trail path to Arvada was empty. There was no one else there except for us few people and our wagons. All we could see was the foothills that stayed green as if forever in the distance, and with the cool breeze, just short of a slight wind, the journey became somehow easier to deal with, especially now, since Emily was better and the worst looked to be over and done.

Mr. Hawkins and Jacob took two horses to go hunting. Fresh meat for the evening dinner would be welcomed and well deserved for all who remained with the small band of travelers.

"Mama, stop, listen!" Katherine exclaimed. "I hear a sound, like rushing water. Maybe it's a stream! Or a river! Oh, I hope it's water. It would be so nice to have a bath." Katherine became more excited.

"We have been on the trail for the longest time. May we go see? It doesn't sound far off. We will be careful, and we'll come straight back to tell you if we find anything. Oh, may we, Mama?" Katherine pleaded, holding her hands up as if she were praying.

"You young'un's be careful, now. We have had enough of the shenanigans that happen to you all when you go off like this. Jakie, you go along with Katherine and Katey, and you watch out for the girls. The wagons are keeping on so you keep watch for us and don't lose sight. If you get lost or lag behind, your father will be upset that I told you it was permitted to take another adventure."

The oxen caught wind of the smell of water and started on their own way, just as the children did.

The oxen were headed for water, where ever that was.

Isobel held on as the team decided they were going for a drink as if it was the most important thing in the world. As it most probably was. Isobel sighed and held the reins as tightly as she held Emily but she could not control their direction.

The children ran across the grassy landscape to see where and what the sound was, and like Katherine had hoped, it was water. It looked like a stream of about twenty feet in breath and only about three feet in depth. Katherine couldn't keep from jumping in and dousing herself with the fresh mountain waters, and it was freezing!

"Katherine you're all wet now. Mama's not going to be happy with you when she gets here," Jakie said, crossing his arms.

Katherine's teeth were chattering. "That's fine, Jacob Summers junior. She is not going to be happy with you, either. You are supposed to be watching us and keeping us out of mischief, so you might as well jump in too," Katherine reminded.

That is all it took for Jakie to jump into the cold waters and soak himself to the bone, clothes and all. He did not even bother to remove his shoes and socks. The children were all drenched to their very being. They enjoyed every freezing bit of that stream.

After refreshing themselves for a short while, they reminded themselves that the wagons were still on the trail and they had to get back. Shortly after their bath, Isobel arrived with the wagon and a very thirsty team and they would need to get their fill.

"Jakie, would you run ahead and tell the others about what we found? You are so much faster than we are and you will reach them sooner," Isobel said trying to get him to go while the ladies enjoyed the water a while longer.

"Why do I have to go? Why don't you girls go?" Jakie questioned and whined.

"Because I raised you to be a gentleman," Isobel reminded climbing down from the wagon with Emily.

"No, it's all right Isobel. I will go with Jakie. Come on," Katey said reluctantly.

Katey crawled out onto the sandy bank of the stream and while she tried not to shiver too much, she squeezed as much water from the tail end of her dress as she could. Jakie sat down, took off his shoes, and poured out at least a good pan full of water and silt.

Both of them peeled off their socks and rung them out then just threw them over their shoulders. They put their shoes back on, then ran as fast as they could to catch up to the wagon party. After a while they caught up with the wagons.

Mrs. Hawkins said, "Children you are a sight. How did you get so wet?"

Breathless, Jakie told the happy news.

"I wonder how come our teams did not smell the water?" Mrs. Hawkins asked. Jakie said, "The wind shifted. Our team almost missed it too."

Right then and there everyone steered their wagons back to the stream.

Soon, everyone enjoyed the water and their long deserved baths. It did not take long for the ladies to find out how cold the water was, because after seeing Isobel, Katey and Emily in the water, all the other women jumped in as well, clothes and all.

"Jacob is off on a hunt with Mr. Hawkins. Maybe tonight, we will have fresh fish and fresh meat for supper." Mrs. Hawkins said floating on her back.

"Oh, that would be nice," Isobel said." I am so tired of corn dodgers and hardtack."

All the wagons were stopped. The teams were lowing to get at the water. Katey and Jakie unhitched them and brought them down stream to drink some healthy water for a change and turn them loose to eat some fresh prairie grasses. The oxen deserved every bit of it.

It was a wonderful sight indeed, to see so many happy people jumping with joy about being clean and watching the wonderful feeling this simple water gave.

But, my goodness it was bone shivering cold.

Chapter 32- Wonder of Wonders!

Another day's journey was done. Another sun came up and gone down once again. The journey was made a little less harsh by the bath in the stream back a piece. They all just jumped right in, clothes and all. It didn't matter, and besides it was a good way to wash their clothing and stay cool while on the trip, at least for a short few hours.

Everyone was feeling fine and refreshed. The teams were watered and they had a chance to eat fresh grass and fine roots from the stream banks. Now with the teams rested, they were raring to go again. The oxen teams were so happy for the opportunity to drink cool clear water and eat some new grasses, they bellowed and swung their heads from side to side just like they did at the beginning of the journey.

It was almost as if they knew things were better and the trip was almost over.

The day got better as they all went along. Mr. Hawkins spotted a rider coming up to their wagon party further up the trail. It was wagon master, Biggs. He had taken the train up trail a few days to steer clear of the whooping cough, and rested the families while they waited for the Summers and the rest to catch up.

"We are up about six miles on this trail," Gridley Biggs said. "I was hoping you would be coming up soon. How's the little one, Mrs. Summers? She come through it alright?"

"See for yourself. She's right here," Isobel said, with a pleased and relieved smile.

Emily popped her head out of the blanket she was wrapped in and showed Mr. Biggs a very happy grin.

"That's the way I like to see the children. Happy as a new filly in fresh straw. We will be at the camp in short time. The others will be glad to hear the news. I am going to ride up and tell them I found you. You all keep going on this stretch of trail and you will be there in no time at all."

Biggs rode off at an excited gallop with a yelping yahoo. You could tell he was glad they were fine and the train would be all together again. Somehow, you could tell his conscience was relieved to know nothing bad happened to anyone; especially the children. He could not bear that again.

He felt like a failure and he let everyone down

when Mrs. Samuelson was killed. He was going to do everything he could in his abilities as wagon master to keep every soul in this train safe and far from harm.

The day was one of the best ever on the journey. Today would reunite all the members of the train and wives and mothers could be together with husbands and children once more. The reunion was a teary eyed event. Hugs and handshaking went on and on. The children were playful and happy once again. The wagon family was together.

Smiles and laughter were found throughout the entire wagon train. The wondering if any more disease was going to catch up with them was nowhere near their thoughts. It was truly a day of celebration. So they did just that.

The men caught some fresh meat. The musicians of the train took out their instruments and tuned up to play.

The women, as usual, prepared a mouthwatering and delicious supper, and the children were busy helping with chores where they were needed. Everyone was happy doing their part.

Soon, the evening came and it was time to eat and dance and listen to the foot stomping music provided by the talented musicians. Turkey in the Straw, Aunt Roadie, and The Virginia Reel were just a few of the tunes they played. Everyone danced about like they all had a little too much Who Hit John. Although, to the contrary, they were all just very glad folk, knowing they would make California within just a few weeks. The journey was just a short time to done.Only once before did they ever feel like this was going to happen and only a few times before did they feel like a real family. The bad times were gone, at least for the time being.

They knew the rest of the trail was going to be slow and treacherous. The hardest part of the trip was still to come.

The Utah territories and the Nevada desert territories were the hottest and the most miserable part of the land, and in order to get to California, the families knew they were to cross it in the driest and hottest part of the year.

This was not going to be an easy time.

Chapter 33-
Decisions on the Other Side

The long, rugged trip across the plains and the Great Saddle of the Rocky Mountains was coming to an end. They reached the summit and looked out to the horizon. Everyone could see for miles. There, laying before them, was the beauty and desolate harshness of the vast Utah territory and the even more endless Utah desert.

The Utah desert was well known, famous in fact, for its salt filled silica sand, the type of sand that would eat right through a wagon wheel axle and bracing as if it were a dog gnawing a bone. The metal rim along the outside if each wagon wheel was no match for the corrosive minerals that lay in that sand. The alkali deposits located in much of the water was the scourge of the trail, and the oxen teams had to be kept from drinking any water from the poisonous water holes.

The proof of this plight could be seen along the trail in the numerous ruins of wagons that did not make it due to mechanical breakdown. The skeletons of animals that died of thirst or starvation due to the lack of needed, essential water and fresh grasses were scattered along the trail. Bones, flies and decayed bodies of these animals proved that this was not a region to be taken for granted. It is pretty much common knowledge if you lose your stock you will not have much time left.

Water was going to be more important now than ever before, so a decision needed to be made.

The wagons stopped at the command of Wagon Master Biggs. He called together the citizens of the train to hold a sort of train town meeting. It was a perfect day. The sun was now at the noon peak. It was high in the sky and staring down on everyone. A smooth breeze was gently rushing over the weather beaten skin of each of the people. It was a good day to discuss this difficult subject. This desert held true to its name.

"The Utah territory that we are about to cross is one of the worst sections of land on the face of the earth. Only one other is worse, and that is yet to come. The Utah desert is full of sagebrush and dry heat.

Many pioneers have traveled over its surface and lived. Many have gone before us completing a successful journey, making it with little or no

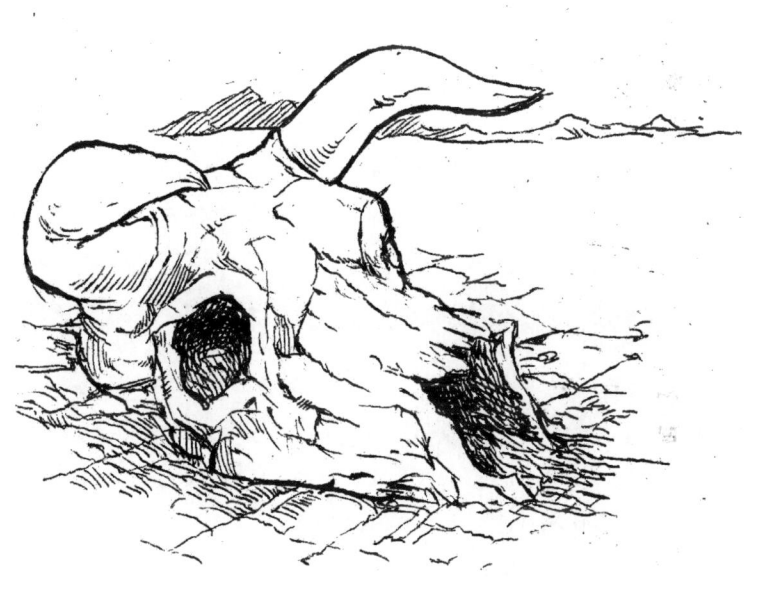

problem. We will travel by night.

Night will provide us with coolness without the heat of the sun cooking our flesh, not to mention what it will do to our teams," Mr. Biggs said.

"What about Indians? The Piute and Shoshone are notorious for attacking wagons at night. What do we do with them and how do we deal with them for passage without any conflict? We only have enough guns and ammunition for our hunting, not for any fight with hostile Indians," Mr. Hawkins said.

A grumble of concern rose from the meeting.

Jacob added his comments, "It looks to me, that in every way, we have no choice but to travel by night. We are so close to California, and if I have anything to do about it, we are going to make it there by hook or by crook. We will have the stars to help guide us so we will have light for the trail. The teams will last longer and the children will be out of danger from sun attack. We, too, will hold up all the better for this decision. We will deal with the Indians if we happen to come across any. To be honest, I don't think we will have any thing to worry about."

The women had their say as well.

"If we must travel by night, then so be it. The children must be looked after and kept safe from harm as best we can do for them. So, let's rest here and then we can take the first miles off the trail. And besides, since this desert is so dangerous during the day, this would be a good opportunity to freshen the water and make sure the teams have a chance to eat green grass instead of desert brush."

Everyone agreed.

The breeze that was caressing each face in the group was suddenly gone, replaced with a warm wind that felt like it was filled with sandpaper.

As was the usual, there was work to be done. The more prepared for this stretch the wagon party was, the easier the trip was bound to be.

They spent the day working as hard as they possibly could. Soon, they would be resting and relaxing in the cooler weather of the higher altitudes of the mountains before they headed into the desert. The wagons needed to get to a shaded area that Mr. Biggs knew about. They had to travel as fast as the teams would go in the night air so the next day's sun did not catch them unguarded.

Sundown came and the wagon party heard the all too familiar call from Mr. Biggs. "HEY YOOOOO!"

They were off for one of the most treacherous trails they had ever traveled.

Chapter 34-
The Great Nevada Trail

The hot, Utah desert sun went down over the western horizon. The colors were beautiful. The blends of crimson red and deep indigo blue, with a hint of pink and yellows mixed together, lit a fire all over the western sky. The sun's rays reached out to touch everything and the crystal beams of light caressed the dusk lighted sky. The aroma of the flowers that only bloomed at night floated through the night air to give an air of perfume that was only equaled by the great glass arboretum where wonderful plants from all over the world were kept on display, back in Minneapolis.

Everything was calmer, and more peaceful. It felt like the trail straightened out for the night's journey.

It was like it knew the pioneers had to make the trip as safely as possible, and the natural things of the desert were there to help in any way they could. Before they could begin the time across the desert, they needed to cross the Colorado River. This was something they were not unfamiliar. Crossing a river, any river, by wagon ferry was long and time taking.

The heat of the day's sun was transformed into a much kinder and gentler temperature. The daytime was over, but now, it did not matter. Everyone was happier and less stressed about the heat. Even the teams were moving with more lightness in their stride. The night gently handed the travelers a certain air of welcoming, which made the trip feel easier despite the moonlit darkness

The night wild life were out and trying to find their meals. The howling coyotes could be heard for miles. Owls winged by in silence, and the sounds of smaller critters scurrying among the brush alongside the trail made the night time sound like a tiny busy street. As busy a street in the desert could sound.

A cool, late night summer breeze greeted the wagons. It evened out the inner fire that lay just underneath each of our skins. That burn didn't bother anyone any longer. It was replaced with enthusiasm and encouragement that the trip was more than halfway complete.

The desert at night is one of the most beautiful places we ever saw. The colors of the desert night along with a mixture of purples and soft browns of the sandy dirt left us with a sense we never felt before along any trail. For the entire time, the rustling of the sagebrush and tumbleweeds turning and rolling

across the trail was entertaining.

We started counting them and kept counting as many as we could for the rest of time in the desert. It helped make the time pass over the many hours.

The desert went on forever and seemed it would not end. The wagon train had to cross this endless part of the journey and reach the Humboldt Trail as soon as they could to beat the late August heat. The Nevada territory was the worst. The wrecked remnants of wagons and belongings buried partially in the sand along the trail were strong evidence the citizens of the wagon train needed to make a fast trip of the region. The rusted wagon wheel rims, and furniture hinges, the rotted old wood from wagons that could not make it for one reason or the other, and the skeletons of mules, horses, and oxen lying along the side of the trail, were all signs we needed to pay attention and be aware of the possibilities.

Mr. Biggs rode to each of the wagons to tell them to travel tightly together and not wander, even in the slightest degree. No one could afford to get lost out here, especially at night. The trail would end soon at a bluff about ten miles up the trail. There, they could rest during the day and beat the scorch of the sun.

In a few short hours daylight would come back and this time it would be welcome. The wagons stopped together along the lea side of the bluffs Mr. Biggs scouted. We had to be able to rest out of the sun, but it was short lived.

The Summers family, the Hawkins, and all the rest were setting the camp when they heard a most ferocious sound. The growl was nothing like a bear or bobcat.

This was louder and sounded like a woman screaming for help.

This sound came from the biggest cat that roamed this desert, a Puma, a Mountain Lion, a Mountain Ghost. Not only was this Puma hungry, it, more than likely, caught wind of the Oxen teams. It was too near for anyone to be careless. The howl was heard once more.

Everyone of the men brought out rifles and ammunition. The teams were now more valuable than ever, so a guard was placed with men watching over four strategic points closely surrounding the animals. The woman and children huddled together in each of the wagons, wondering and listening for that fearful howl.

Even Sam, the Summers hunting dog, was on the watch. This would be something no one would ever forget.

Chapter 35- Showdown

Just before daybreak the desert suddenly chilled – not with any wind or freezing snows, but with a feeling. Three more men with rifles and pistols increased the watch around the wagons oxen teams. Every wagon had at least one man armed with a rifle to watch for any predators that were lurking.

In Minnesota, there was nothing like this noise. The people did not know what to expect. No one had ever heard anything like the scream that echoed over the desert landscape. The women and children huddled in the wagons for safety, while the men of the train were not going to get any sleep that day. Every man was armed and on the lookout for something. What it was, they did not know.

Being from the backwoods areas of the upper Midwest, they knew about bears and badgers, and had even heard wolverines howl, but this sound was terrifying. When this creature screamed, it sent the coldest of chills down your back, and would start on one side of your body and go right through you.

Every eye was sharpened and every ear was listening. Some of the men even said they could smell a critter from a mile off. The only thing that made this difficult was none of them had taken a bath for several days, not since Katherine found the stream for them to bathe in.

Something was close. The oxen and the other teams of mules, including the livestock, were getting nervous and fidgety. Sam, the Summer's dog, stood up, bared his sharp teeth and growled a low growl. The dog was ready, but for what, not even Sam knew.

The men readied the rifles and cocked the triggers of each of the rifles and pistols, just in case the puma attacked without being seen. The shadows cracking through the daybreak made it very difficult to see what direction the noise was coming from. Another, much louder, screaming howl was heard. This time, it was much closer.

Sam jumped down from the back of the Summer's wagon and carefully made his way through the legs of the men who stood point of the teams. He lifted his nose upward to catch the scent of this creature.

There was nothing that Sam did not put his keenly trained nose across. Wheels, bushes, peoples legs and shoes, everything got smelled.

Sam walked around to the other side of the oxen teams to see what it was.

Hunting dogs are known for their sense of smell, far more than their eyesight, and Sam was no exception. Blue Tick hounds have been known to grab a scent from two miles off and then track that scent down until they relentlessly find the prey and tree the critter. In the past, Sam was known to have killed the largest and fiercest of raccoons or take on a bear in his time, but he was just as tired as the rest of the people in the train. Could he do the job if he was needed?

A loud, painful, yell was heard from one of the men. Everyone quickly looked over.

"Oh, I did it this time. I stood too close to one of the oxen. He shook his head and gored me with a one of those horns. It doesn't look serious, but it burns somethin' awful. I'll be right as rain in a while," Mr. Haggerty said, groaning as he bent over.

"You go back to the wagons and get looked after. Isobel will get that taken care of. It is lucky it looks like you only got a scrape," Jacob said examining the wound.

Mr. Haggerty headed back to the wagons.

He clearly was not ready for what happened next.

The creature screamed one more howl and pounced on top of Mr. Haggerty as he was headed back. The smell of Mr. Haggerty's blood was all it took to bring the big cat in for a meal. Mountain Lions have been known to attack Indians and drag off small children, and even take on game larger than themselves.

Sam ran as fast as he could, barking and growling at the same time. Sam leaped into the air and landed in the middle of the desert lion, knocking him off Mr. Haggerty.

The Puma backed off, swiping at Sam with his two inch claws. He hunched down, baring his scraggly and sharp looking teeth. The cat's ears were down and the big cat was ready to pounce. Seconds went by, the cat suddenly lunged at Sam. Sam was just out of reach. Sam growled and barked louder and lunged back at the big cat while the men dragged Mr. Haggerty out of harms way.

The cat growled and leaped into the air and landed on Sam. Sam, growling and ready, wrestled with the cat and bit the cats neck. They turned over and over, each tumbling over and through sharp brambles and cactus thorns. The battle was fierce, neither willing to give up or retreat. And as quickly as it began, it ended.

Sam managed to back off a short distance, took a breath and, as if from out of nowhere, the air was cut with the sound of Piute Indian arrows that found their target in the huge cat.

Sam escaped with a few scrapes and claw marks, as well as a few cactus needles, but the big cat was not so fortunate.

There it lay on the desert sand. The men were not able to get a shot off for fear they would hit Sam, but when the opportunity arose, death came to the big cat. But what happened? They did not kill this cat, yet, there it lay with two arrows sticking from its ribs.

The men ran to where the big cat was and noticed something or someone coming from behind a tall cactus.

From out of the darkness it was a single, tall Indian man. He was walking towards them holding a bow and a few arrows in his buckskin quiver. His demeanor was quiet, and he seemed friendly.

This was his kill and he was coming to claim the cat for his family.

The Great Spirit had given him this victory today.

Chapter 36-
The Guide

The men, with their mouths wide open, just stood watching. The Indian, with a sort of sign language, told the men that the cat was his as his reward from the Great Spirit. It was the Great Spirits way of saying: I give you this gift for the spirit of your young son. The cat's pelt would provide many nights of warmth and many days of cover from the heat of the desert sun.

Placing his bow and arrows on the ground, the Indian knelt over the big cat and began to chant in song. He was thanking the Great Spirit for bringing this cat to him.

His song went on for several minutes. He stopped and then said something to the cat. He knelt down and yanked the arrow from the cats ribs, held it up to the sky with both hands, and then snapped it in half. It was as if he freed the spirit of the cat from the arrow so the cat could also regain its dignity when it went into the spirit world on the other side and was welcomed by the Great Spirit.

We had never seen any ritual like it.

"Mama, do you think he is sad or happy?" Katherine asked.

"I think this man is happy, because his journey is over. I also think this man is sad because the memory of this cat and the pelt will be a reminder of the son he lost. This man, for his penance, will wear the skin of the cat for a very long time," Isobel explained.

Jakie asked, "Mama, how come you know so much about Indians?"

"Your grandmother was the wisest woman I ever knew. If she didn't know about it, it was never there to begin with. Your grandmother taught me everything I know about herbs and healing. She told me that the Indians taught her about spirit magic and told her the ways of many different things," Isobel said.

"But Preacher Thompson said the Indians are heathens and …" Katherine was interrupted.

"Let me tell you right now, daughter, even Preacher Thompson said there are things about the heavens that have yet to be explained. He was the most wide-eyed and open minded man I ever met.

He always looked out for new miracles, as he liked to call them. He saw things so special and so unusual that mere people would never understand

how they got there or why they always worked. He was a man of great faith. I think that great faith brought him many great gifts."

Isobel continued. "Preacher Thompson was a good man in the eyes of the Indians back home. He respected them, and they him. He was the one who told your grandmother when they needed her help for healing. He spoke their language. That is how well he knew them."

As Isobel explained further, the children watched the Indian lift the large limp dead cat up as if it was a rag doll and drape it across his back. The cat looked like a sack of potatoes just dangling there.

"Mama wait!" Katherine blurted out. "The man fell."

Isobel and the others ran to his side, pulled the heavy cat away from his body and suddenly noticed how thin the man was.

"Jacob you get some water. Jakie, Katherine, and you too Katey get the robe. It will take the three of you to get it here. Mrs. Hawkins would you please get my poultice bag? This man is sick from starvation. He must have been hunting this cat for days without any food."

Isobel and a few other ladies helped make the Indian comfortable right there on the desert floor. He was too big to lift up and she wasn't about to touch that cat. Something was still in its eyes.

No matter how much we realized that it was dead, it still had an eerie look to it. A kind of spookiness in its eyes which were still open.

The children brought the heavy buffalo robe to their mother and placed it on the man just as they were instructed.

Within a few minutes, the robe had done its magic once again. The man awoke and sat up. He was dazed and a little afraid, but thankful. Jacob gave him a few sips of water and Mr. Biggs handed him a few strips of salted beef.

The Indian watched everyone around him, looking at the crowd of white people standing and helping him. He became nervous when something told Katherine to hold out her hand in friendship. Jacob did the same and so did the rest of the men in the watch party.

They put down their guns and helped the man to his feet.

The Indian man looked around to find the cat he must bring back to his family, when he noticed the robe. He held it in front of him with both strong arms outstretched towards Isobel and motioned that he knew of this robe and who had given it to her. He knew the stories of the great medicine woman who saved the Great Chief's son.

In sign language, the Indian said, "Thank you for saving my life."

Chapter 37-
To Carson City

The Indian man stumbled a little as he tried to walk towards the camp with the help of two of the men. They wrapped his arms around their necks and shoulders, supporting him on each side, while trying to keep him covered with the buffalo robe.

The children peered out from the covers of the wagons as the tallest Indian, or man for that matter, they had ever seen, walked quietly to the campfire. He was tired, it was obvious he was weak from being without food and nourishment for many days, but he seemed a proud man. You could tell in the way he stood and stride with his long legs, each arm trying to hold up a silent strength as he walked with the men.

His trousers were a woven cloth with a beaded ceremonial belt to hold them up. His quiver of arrows was hand made with ornate and finely polished small stones. They glimmered in the sunlight.

When he arrived at the wagon, he said some words none of us understood, and smiled. He took papa's forearm in his hand and papa took his in the same manner. They shook arms, I guess you could say. The Indian man said something to Papa and looked at Mama, and then he gave the robe back to our mother.

Mama, without a flinch, took the robe and put it back in its place in the wagon.

The man looked about to find a place to rest, and settled into a spot nearby the wagons and the campfire and began the job of readying the big cat for his journey home.

After skinning the lion, the Indian took the puma pelt and rolled it up to make it easy to carry on his back. No one knew how long, or how far he had to go, to get back home. All we knew was that he was not going to part without that pelt.

The time to rest was here, and although it was daytime, and we were supposed to be on the trail in a few hours, those who were not frightened from of the visitor rested. Mr. Haggerty staggered to the resting place of the man who had saved his life. The Indian man sat up holding the big cat skin close.

Mr. Haggerty simply reached out with a hand of friendship and thanks. They both knew, deep down,

that this was going to be a whole different type of knowing than either one had ever been accustomed.

For both Indian and white, the terrible stories that preceded both races were about to come to a truthful end. They were to both find that stories, and especially terrible tales of man against man, race against race, are spread like a dry fire by fearful and greedy men, but not by men of honor, regardless of skin color or beliefs.

Everyone almost forgot the oxen and the other animals had been rigged for over two hours and each team was in need of water. Everyone needed water. It would be a blessing to find another stream like the one three weeks ago, but out in the dry desert, it was as if they would never taste a wild moving stream ever again. The trains drinking water was in short supply and no one knew where the nearest water could be found. Not even Mr. Biggs knew.

After the days events, night all came and helped ease the character of the day. The evening's coolness brought a steady breeze and the knowing the time for another journey along the trail and along the darkened cliffs with their tall, wind carved rocks, that were a part of the desert.

The men were discussing the shortage of water when the Indian called out and motioned the men to come closer. They walked to him and he gave a sign that said he could bring them to water and it was not far.

Each one of the men was perplexed by what the

big Indian was trying to say, but just as the children had once before, they figured out what the man was saying, just as they had done back at Fort Kearney.

"Everyone, he is saying he knows where waters is," Katherine said.

The Indian man knew that Katherine knew what he was saying and smiled. He motioned for the wagons to follow him and they would have all the clear water they could want.

He gathered his bow and arrows, then draped the rolled and tanned hide across his shoulders and began to lead the wagon party up the trail to what was to be a welcome sight. This was the beginning of the Carson Trail and the beginning to the end of their journey.

Or was it… really?

Chapter 38-
Water Water Everywhere

For two more nights, the wagon train traveled on the Humboldt trail through the Nevada desert and territory. The Indian guided them over many areas of desolate and coarse sandy lands. Still no water. Nothing was to be found anywhere near the trail. The only sign of anything resembling water was a distant thunderstorm that roared far behind them on a trail they might have mistakenly wandered from.

The teams were getting slower. The people were beginning to stagger from lack of water. It was needed, and needed now. The water that was still in the barrels, was rationed for so many things – a little for cooking, a little for drinking.

As much as possible was given to the teams. None of it was for bathing. It was down to the bottoms of every barrel.

Still no sign of any water, and it did not look like there was going to be any.

Jakie wanted to know the name of the Indian, so he went up ahead to find out.

He ran up and tugged on the Indian's buckskin trouser leg, and looked at him eye to eye.

"My name is Jakie? What is your name?"

The Indian just looked down at Jakie and smiled as if he was giving approval to his own son. He didn't say a word.

Jakie tried again, only this time he tried what he thought would pass for sign language.

"My name is Jakie. I am the son of the medicine woman, Isobel."

His words about the medicine woman sparked something in the big man's face. He knew these words, he heard the magical words and he stopped. He knelt down and cupped Jakie's face in his large hand, and motioned something that meant he knew of the great gifts Isobel had been given, and how she saved the son of the Great Chief. Because his life had been spared, he would return the gift of life to the rest.

He still said nothing. He did not say a single word. Jakie would not have understood what he said anyway.

He only used the sign language.

Somehow Jakie knew everything was going to be all right. The Indian was an honorable man, and one we all grew to trust that.

Jakie reached out and took the man's hand and shook it like the way Preacher Thompson used to do after the sermon on Sunday morning, with kindness and firmness that could mean bless you.

Jakie ran back to his family wagon and told his family what he'd done.

"Papa, I spoke with the Indian," he said catching his breath.

"You did what?" Katherine asked. "You know Papa's going to skin your hide."

Papa gave Katherine a look that said, "excuse me, daughter" and asked Jakie. "What did you say boy?"

"I asked him what his name is. He didn't say anything. He motioned some sign words.

I got the feeling when he smiled that we were going to arrive at water real soon," Jakie said with confidence.

"Uh huh, and I am the Queen of Spain, "Katherine said.

"Now, you hold your tongue, young lady," Jacob said.

Katherine quickly held her hand over her mouth so she wouldn't say anything out of turn again. She took her father's suggestion to mean the literal.

"Why do you think this, Jakie? We have not seen natural water for over two weeks," Papa said.

Jakie simply said, "Because the Indian told me we

would be alright. All of us will."

The boy went round back of the wagon and jumped onto their wagon rear gate to rest a bit.

Isobel and Jacob both turned to each other and shook their heads in wonderment at their son.

"He does come up with some tales," Jacob said.

"Yes, it looks like he gets that from his father," Isobel chuckled.

The trail was winding on and on as the starlit night hours went by. Suddenly, the teams bolted and started to quicken the pace as only oxen teams can do.

"Papa!" Katherine screamed with surprise. "What are they doing?"

"They smell water! Hang on children."

All the teams of all the wagons smelled the water. It was just over a small rise and the animals knew exactly where to go.

The Indian man jumped atop one of the teams of oxen and rode it all the way to the Humboldt River, whooping and hollering like nothing the wagon citizens ever witnessed before.

He waved his bow and arrows high into the sky as if the was yelling out a prayer of thanks to the Great Spirit for bringing the water, and for helping him repay his life's gift.

When we arrived, the teams were unhitched and we let them jump right into the river. The shook their large heads and drank and a few laid down in the water.

The Humboldt was full of water. It was a gentle running current, with current eddies near the shore gentle enough to jump right into without fear of being whisked away and lost down river.

The teams had to be brought back from drinking so much all at once. They would get a type of water stomach ache from being dehydrated. Drinking too much water after so long can lay out an oxen right fast.

"Not all at once. Just a little at a time," Mr. Biggs told everyone. "We don't want to lose any of them." The excitement of the water in the river was incredible. To have water to drink and to cook with again and mostly to bathe in was a blessing and a gift from above.

The Indian was in the water as well. After all, it was our new friend who guided them to this oasis.

He deserved to take a dip. We ail discovered right quick that this river was colder than any we had experienced before.

Everyone was in the river all at once, splashing and diving under the water and taking whole mouthfuls of water, and then spitting the water out like the fountain back in Garden City. It was a sight. The watery celebration went on for hours. Nobody wanted to get out of the river. Some members of the train just sat in the water and stayed there, smiling enjoying themselves.

The time drew on into almost dawn and with everyone cooled down and the teams watered, the

train could come to calm again. All the wagons had full water barrels once again . All the canteens were full.

Many of the women put water into anything that would hold it without spilling too much. Some of the men dipped into the water one more time with their hats, scooping up as much as the hat would hold and then poured them over their heads for one more cool shower.

They did not know when they might get another opportunity like this any time soon.

Soon after the revelry and all, Jakie saw the Indian leaving.

"Wait!" Jakie called out.

Jakie and the rest of the children, all soaking wet, ran to him and asked as best they could.

"Where are you going?"

The big man signed, more like a pointing to the horizon in the distance, that he was going back home to his village and to his people.

Isobel thought for a moment and told the children to get the man a canteen of water,and some jerky.

"Jakie get your fathers hunting knife and get some help with the medicine robe and bring it too."

The children did as they were told. Katherine gave the man the canteen of water. Katey gave him the jerky.

Isobel took the knife from Jakie.A few other children helped with the special buffalo robe.

She laid it out and cut a piece of the robe off, and

both Isobel and Jacob handed it to the man who had saved them all from death.

This courageous man knew of its power. He smiled, and hand signed , "Thank you."

He gently held both of their arms in a show of friendship and unity. He saw Jakie standing there and tousled Jakie's hair and smiled at him.

He turned and walked off into the desert.

We never saw this brave man again.

The Pioneer Journey

Going West

Book Three

Chapter 39- Into Carson

A week went by after our meeting with our new friend at the Humboldt River. We must have covered some one hundred mile. We were all wondering when our next stop would be and where it would be. Mr. Biggs came riding up at a full gallop passing each wagon with an exciting announcement.

"Two days ride to Carson! Two days ride to Carson!"

He rode all the way to the back of the train and then turned his horse and galloped back to the point of the train.

"Good news, good news!"

At the front of the wagon train Mr. Biggs called out a YOOOO, and all the wagons came to a stop.

He called out for everyone to come to a meeting of the train to hear what he had to say. Families gathered at the head of the wagons.

"This is good news Mr. Biggs," Mr. Hawkins said.

"Yes it is, but what next? What kind of town is Carson? We have heard of many exciting things and about wild goings-ons in the town. What should we expect?" Mrs. Hawkins asked.

The excited children began to figit when they heard telling of great streets and stores with mercantile goods. Goods none had seen forever so long.

"I heard there are stores in the town where they have jars filled to the brim with candies and sweets you can enjoy for days. They have a drink for children called soda water and sarsaparilla. It tickles your nose, and you can put different color juices in it and it tastes like that juice only it sparkles."

Katherine argued, "Jakie, you have not heard any such thing."

"Yes I did. Jimmy Haggerty told me so," Jakie replied.

"How does he know? He hasn't been to Carson, has he?" Katherine argued.

"Katherine! You are becoming quite free with your tongue lately. What has gotten into you? You behave now. You hear me?" Isobel scolded.

Katherine held her tongue and dropped her head feeling a bit ashamed.

"Two days hard ride if we want to make it and have some time to rest," Mr. Biggs said to everyone.

"It will be the last hard drive before we make the trip northward and up the Beckwourth trail. We must make the pass before the cold comes. In my experience you can never tell when the pass snows will come. We do not need to have that difficulty hinder us, especially now that we are so close. We will only spend two days in Carson; just enough to re supply and rest the teams. The base of the pass is steep and difficult to ford. The teams and us have to be at our best.

But I tell you this, after we reach the summit, the land is so green and so rich with beauty, you will know why we all made this journey."

Mr. Biggs got back on his horse. Everyone went back to the wagons and went to the whip with a snap of each rod, the animals started up, and they were on the way

An unknown finger of the Humboldt River was the trail. It gave a steady supply of water and a good pathway for the train to follow straight into Carson.

Just like before, when we started out across the great desert of the Utah territory, a great excitement and wonder arose in each of us. The questions each made the journey into Carson seem shorter.

The two days went by quick. And before they knew it the town of Carson surrounded them. The shops were all around them. As they continued to drive the wagons through the streets, the safe sense of wonder was dwindling to a feeling of uneasiness. What they found in the town was mercantiles. Large ones where they could replenish the supplies they needed and then some. They also found a more than wild, mining town, filled to the outskirts with greed and men who had not been among civil people for a long time. The saloons and ill reputed opium dens littered the main streets and back alleys throughout the town. There was strange oily stink to the air, and as we passed by these places we saw men staggering along the wooden side walks and dirt lined streets. Some men were laying there in the middle with a blankness to their faces. It was not a place we wanted to be.

Mr. Biggs guided the wagons to the outer north side of town and stopped the train. He called for another meeting. He warned them that the town was not as he remembered. It was a kind and gentle family filled town, but not any more. Ever since the silver strike in nearby Virginia City, prospectors came from all over to seek their fortune, and turned the town into a wild and lawless place. He also warned them, this is nothing compared to what they were to go through next. Truckee Meadows was just up the trail about a days ride. After that, it was all or nothing to California just over the Sierra trail known as the Beckwourth pass.

Chapter 40-
The Last Stretch

The territory of Nevada was known as the most liberally tolerant place to a persons personal considerations any man or woman could ever reside, east of the Sierra Nevada mountains.

The town of Carson was no exception. The miners who toiled in the dark deepness of the silver mines were not the ones making the money in the region: it was the store keepers who sold supplies to those wayfaring wealth seekers, who planned to stake. or had staked a claim among all the other hundreds of men, that made the riches. And they made it by charging high prices for food and tools and other worldly commodities needed. Whatever money the miners made, may well have just been handed straight into the hands of the owner of the mercantile and more easily into the hands of the saloon keeper: not to mention the occasional thief, who would think nothing of either robbing you in broad daylight, or jumping your claim. However, the town was not lawless, it was just much less, inhibited, as they would put it, than others.

Between Virginia City over the range and Truckee Meadows, the wholesome ideals of any God fearing man woman, or child was short lived if they decided to reside in Carson for any lengthy period of time.

If a man could put up with the drunkenness of most of the miners, the solicitations of con men, and the soulless–ness of many of the population, he might find the area a right fine place to live. The land was cheap for homesteading. The weather was torturous hot at times, and mild in others. It was after all, a direct route to California and her gold fields, and a direct, four hard days trip to the magical city of San Francisco.

One cannot forget the wonder of the almost mythological blue waters of the Pacific Ocean. Carson was a perfect place to go away from, or to simply pass through on the way to better digs.

I heard say from one gentleman writer named Mark Twain, *"Carson City is not fit for man nor beast I suppose that is why miners and saloon keepers live here."* The Summer's party was encamped at the northern road out of town. The wagons were grouped closely together and the citizens did not leave the encampment for fear of who knows what, might happen.

It was known of Carson miners that if they had not seen a woman of the female persuasion in a long time they would actually propose deals of partnership in the ownership of their claim staked mines, to Fathers passing through with their daughters, if they would allow them to marry right then and there, as long as the daughter was of marrying age.

Only a few took the offers. Many Fathers ended up penniless and so did their daughters, much less the unfortunate miner if the father did not shoot him.

Needless to say, none of the Summers party encountered anything like that.

The day brought chores and preparations of greasing wheel hubs and food replenishment. They had done that a thousand times before. At least it seemed that way. They knew they were not done yet and there would be many more times the task would be done again.

But this was the point of departure for either going to the Beckwourth Pass or to head over the High Sierra Range Pass south of Carson, and head to Sacramento. This was the spot where Mr. and Mrs. Hawkins were to split off from the rest. They were going to Sacramento.

"Mr. Biggs, It has surely been a pleasure knowing you. We could not have gotten this far without your help," Mr. Hawkins said. "We don't have much left from the journey except our lives and the clothes on our backs. As for our belongings, well, we can get more when we start up the new store. It will be easy to get deliveries

and supplies."

Mr. Biggs shook hands with Mr. Hawkins and tipped his hat to Mrs. Hawkins. They both smiled with a wish of good luck for the remainder of their journey. The trail road the Hawkins were taking was steep and winding, and if they took their time they would make it in an easy four days. The reward at the end was enormous.

Only a small band of four other wagons went along with the Hawkins family. The rest stayed with the original wagon train to go find their fortunes in the lumber industry and stake their own claims in the gold sluices of the Feather River. Everyone was nervous, and anxious and impatient to arrive all at the same time. But still, no one knew exactly when they would arrive at their new home.

Mr. Biggs did not know for sure, especially this time of season. The river might be rising, this being early autumn now, and the trail in the canyon always under the effects of mining and rock slides. He just could not be sure.

So, onward Mr Biggs headed the train. Continuing on for the next stop at Truckee Meadows, just an easy days ride and then up to the Beckwourth Pass.

Jacob Summers could smell a home cooked meal like it was right there next to him.

He, most of all, wanted to get an axe in his hands for a good days work for a good days pay.

He wanted his children to be safely tucked into their own beds, and he especially wanted Isobel to be safe in her own house once again.

Chapter 41- California!

"You folks remember we must cross the Truckee River before we can continue on," Mr. Biggs said at a trail meeting. "If we are lucky we'll find a low line of water and we can cross at that point. I know we are close. So close you all can get your first taste of California in your teeth. Just be patient, we are only a days ride outside the pass and when we get there we'll have us all a great celebration! So lets get going."

With a hardy whip the oxen teams heaved forward and started off once again to a land of green grasses and taller trees than any of them had ever seen.

So tall in fact a person had to lay down on the ground and then look skyward to even begin to see the tip of the tall redwoods.

"Papa, you think that Big John MacKaskill has ever seen a redwood tree? You reckon he might chop these all down?" Jakie asked.

"You know son, I just don't know. He wasn't one to just chop everything down willy-nilly; he only cut what was needed and left all the pretty trees alone. So if these redwoods are as pretty as people say, I doubt he would touch a single branch on any of them. Sides, there are so many trees left to cut in Canada, he probably will never get to California. Not in my lifetime at any rate."

Jakie continued to look from side to side not seeing tree one except for the ones that lined the high ridge land in the mountains to the west.

"Papa there ain't much here is there? Just more and more scrub oaks and harsh dirt and it's hot too," Jakie said.

"You are a talker today aren't you boy. Why so full of questions?" Jacob asked.

"I have never been to California. I guess my mind is just wandering and wanting to see all the great places we been told about since we left home. Tommy Hawkins said that his Papa said that California has different wild critters and grasses greener than we ever saw before. The farms are bigger than any we knew in Minnesota and the water is so pure and clear you can see plum down

to the very bottom of rivers. He told me the fish are so big it takes two men to land one, and that little children are not allowed to fish cause the fish might mistake them for bait and jump on shore and eat them right up."

"Jake, Tommy Hawkins is pulling your leg. He is telling you a tale. His imagination is working hard too. I don't know about the fish and bait although I have heard tales of salmon and trout so big it takes three days for a family of five to eat just one. How's that for a tale boy?"

Jakie and his Father pulled each others legs all the way down the trail. Exchanging tall tales and trying to outdo each others imagination. Both of them making each story even grander than the one before.

"Papa, we learned in school that California was thought to be a glorious island and it was filled with exotic people from everywhere. Do you think we'll see any of them?" Katherine asked.

"Daughter now that sounds like a tall tale. Your teacher really told you that, huh? I do declare. All I know about California is we will be better off than we were in Minnesota. We can have a bigger house, and I can have more work than I can handle for better wages. And we can have a bigger homestead to raise you children. That is what I know of California."

Isobel looked at Jacob and smiled. This was the most he had talked with the children for some time and he was enjoying every minute and every word.

Just then Katey joined in, "California a beautiful place. It does have tall trees and clear streams and rivers. The cities are wonderful and the stores, oh the stores! You can buy candy five for a penny and the material for sewing is some of the prettiest you will ever see, and someday, yes maybe someday, you will get to see the Pacific Ocean. It is the most beautiful sight you will ever see," then she realized what she was saying and stopped.

"Katey I do not understand how you know so much about California. You have never been there," Isobel said.

"Only in my dreams," Katey said.

The wagons wobbled along the trail and continued to Truckee Meadows and the Truckee River. It wasn't long before they arrived at the biggest small town they had ever seen.

As the train arrived they heard gunfire and hollerin'. Lots of yelling and whoopin and whalin. Lots of loud, out-of-tune, piano music was heard from the saloons they passed.

"It appears that trouble should be the name of this place," Isobel said. "The faster we get across the river the safer I will feel."

"Just hold firm Isobel. Nothing will come of it. Everything will be just fine. I am sure," Jacob tried to reassure her.

Chapter 42- Welcome to the New Home

The wagons crossed the Truckee one by one, carefully into the swift freezing river current. Despite the low water line, the wagon wheels would snag a large rock on the bottom and cause wheels to weaken at the spokes. After all the wagons were back on dry land it was time to grease up the axles once again. Bacon fat and lard were brushed in and out the hubs of each wheel. One by one each wheel was taken off and each axle was greased. The hot desert sun was still a factor in the journey. Yet, everyone agreed to keep going. The weather was cooler and the trail was straight ahead. The only thing that was going to make it even the slightest bit difficult was the climb.

The slope on the northern trail, according to Mr. Biggs, was pretty steep. They might have to unload all their goods from the wagons and that would cause another delay. They thought this could stop them for a day or two. Being so close to California and all they all thought it just wasn't possible to have anything else be in the way. They all sighed and headed on towards the new home.

Mr. Biggs told them all to rest the teams before this last run. It was important the animals get rested up before the pass rises up to meet their feet. The pass is a sudden surge of upward trail that goes up via a pass trail that winds along a long ridge. The grassy high valley trail is the entrance to fortune, safety, and all their dreams coming true.

The wagons traveled on for another several hours. Up, up and more up they went. It was not steep, just a steady climb on the trail. They had already been on trails steeper than this; it was just the excitement and wonder building inside each of them. They were so close, yet so far off.

"Where does this lead Mr. Biggs?" was on everyones' minds. The man who had actually single handedly brought 160 people across the vastness of the prairies and the dangers of the Indian territories, the Rocky Mountains, and most recently the deserts of the Nevada and Utah plains knew it. It was his responsibility to get the wagon train to California. Before everyone knew where they were, the wagon train was called to a sudden stop.

"Where are we Mr. Biggs?" Jacob asked. "What's the matter? Is there something wrong?"

Mr. Biggs sitting tall in his saddle simply gazed

over a great grassy hillside.

"Over that hill is why you all came," He pointed across the field. "Ladies and gentlemen over yonder is California."

Everyone in the train went to see what Mr Biggs was looking at. They stood beside him, looking up at the hillside in the short distance. It was beautiful. The air became quiet with a stillness of awe and amazement.

No one said a word. The smiles that covered each face were a sign that they knew, within a matter of a few more days, new homes and lives were theirs for the asking. A feeling of prosperity and plenty was all around.

The citizens let out a cheer, "Hip hip hoorah, they all yelled."

"Don't start cheering yet. We have far to go and even though the first part of this trail is going as smooth as a baby's backside, we need to rest up and be ready for the last leg. It is and will be where you get your metal tested.

Gather up and let's get to California," Mr. Biggs said.

The wagon party startedn again with a regained enthusiasm. They made it. The landscape was a vast flat and fertile prairie. It stretched out forever. A long stream ran through the center of it all.

A dusting of snow was still on the mountaintops and a cool breeze was wafting in across the plain. They went through this type of prairie before, but

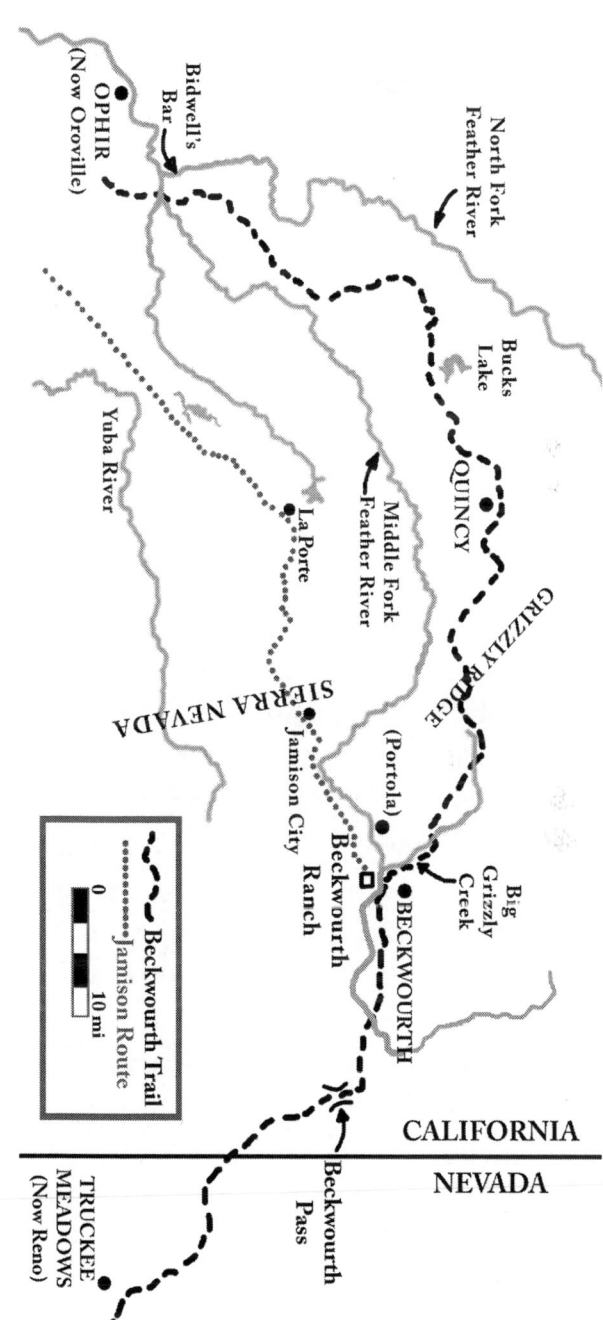

this was different. This was California!

We saw majestic mountainsides, a deep green prairie, we could see the distance glimpse of a tree line, and right in front of us was the most welcomed sight we ever laid our eyes on.

This were the wheel ruts of wagons and families who came before them. The ruts were straight and just deep enough to keep them on a true and dedicated pathway.

The settlers could not be happier, or so they thought.

"Up here are trappers. They come to live here every year to do their trapping and see what comes of it all for them. Some of them don't ever make it out of here alive. It is a very harsh life. So you all mind your wheels and your footing and watch for traps. I don't want any of you getting hurt now." Mr. Biggs cautioned.

A straight trail and flat land, and no harsh heat to bog a person down. The teams were as happy as newborns and the water, oh, the freshness of the new water. It was cold and so clear, from the high melt, it tasted like new snow crystals on your tongue. The Wagon Master knelt down to check something he found on the trail. He placed his hand and fingers along side what he thought was a curious sign. He looked up and peered round the valley. Why was Mr. Biggs being so cautious?

Chapter 43- Getting Supplies

"Mr. Biggs seems anxious about something Mama. What do you think he is thinking about?" Katherine asked.

"I don't know, Katherine. Perhaps you could ask him?"

Katherine ran up to the horse of Mr. Biggs.

"Mr. Biggs?"

"Yes Miss?" Mr. Biggs replied.

"Is there some thing wrong? You seem upset about something. Is everything all right?"

"I cannot tell you right now Miss. Would you ask your Father to see me please?"

"Yes sir I will, right away sir."

Katherine ran as fast as she go to tell her father Mr. Biggs' message.

"Papa Mr. Biggs asked me to tell you to come see him right away."

Jacob gave the willow stick to Jakie and ran up to see what Mr. Biggs wanted.

"Jacob before we got up here on this ridge valley I had only heard about this. Have you noticed the broken and burnt out wagons along the trail?"

"Yes I have but I didn't think anything of it. Why? What's on your mind Mr. Biggs?" Jacob asked.

Mr. Biggs continued with his explanation, "Those wagons aren't there because of being broken down or old. Those are what's left of the families who were here recently. One of those wagons was still smoking from being set aflame."

"Indians?" Jacob asked.

"No, not Indians. They were victims of bandits. Wagon Pirates to be exact. These are people who had met hard times with their own journey and now find it easier to rob travelers of their goods and belongings. They are a worthless lot. They could have made it out here like every other honest pioneer who comes here, but they have chosen a life of thievery and pirating harsher than anyone has ever witnessed.

There are those who have escaped the holdups and robberies. Those folks have lived to tell others of these menaces of the trail. We have to watch out for them. Keep your rifles drawn and tell the others, but, don't cause a stir. Just tell the men, and wives if you would.

We must make it to the first supply depot. The trail stays straight and no climbs from here so I believe we can make it without any problem.

Keep watch. I just think it's odd that all along this journey the only problems we have had were angry bees, our loss of Mrs. Samuelson, and now these trail pirates.

Nary a single Indian has bothered us. A few helped us. How strange that our own people are the only ones to see fit to cause us all bother, and take it on themselves to make our lives, and anyone who they feel needs it, the benefit of their intrusions. It is a true shame."

"I will tell the others," Jacob said, nodded his head, and walked calmly back to inform the other wagons.

The wagons were headed for the supply depot in nearby Beckwourth. This depot, a general supply mercantile of questionable origin was founded by the man himself James Beckwourth. James Beckwourth was a mountain man, a trail blazing trapper of color and responsible for carving the Beckwourth trail all the way to the gold and timber country of central and upper California.

The train arrived unscathed by any deterrents, or pirates, or any other distraction. All the folks were glad to be able to rest for a spell. Still every man carried their rifles and pistols, all carefully on the watch for trail pirates. They were too close to the end of the journey to let any thing happen now. Nothing was going to stop them.

"What do we do next, Mr. Biggs?" Isobel asked.

"The next stop is a timber town called Quincy. We should make it without a problem."

He tried to reassure the citizens of the train, but he knew the trail pirates were going to be an ongoing trouble for the rest of the journey. They must watch closer than ever.

Chapter 44- A Celebration

"Papa? Why do you think that everything here in California is prettier than what we had in Minnesota? I mean, it l just looks that way," Katherine asked her father.

"Daughter, what are you talking about? What do you mean that everything is *prettier*?" Jacob asked back. "You mean to tell me that you think your mother is not as pretty or that your memories of your grandpa and grandma are not as wonderful as when we were in Minnesota? Are your aunts and uncles are a fog in the mist of your imagination?"

Jacob was almost scolding the girl.

"I didn't mean it that way. What I meant was, just because this is California and because we are here now, it just feels fresher. Only because it's new," Katherine added.

Jacob said, "Yes, you are right, and yes, only because it is new. That is the only reason it seems prettier. You wait and see, you don't remember the hard work your mother and me spent to build our farm back in Garden City. It started out to be the prettiest piece of land we ever set our eyes on, but it tooled out rough. The ground was rock hard and the weather was not going to forgive any mistakes we made. We started out with a small cabin, not the big house you knew with the barn and the plowed fields. The whole area was barren. If it weren't for the timberline, we would have spent our first winter in the frozen Minnesota prarie. Garden City was not even a town. There was no school. A few people did come to homestead, and we were all so far away from one another that sometime it appeared we would never see another human being.

For over a year we didn't see anyone until Preacher Thompson's buckboard got loose and the horses wandered into the field. Believe me, he was sight for ragged eyes. I had not known the wonder of seeing another human after a long time, until Preacher Thompson stumbled in after that buckboard.

Your mother had to push me to get me to move.

I was so amazed at seeing another person I was stopped planted right where I was, planted in my shoes.

I remember just standing there staring at this man in black with his round wide brimmed hat with its white band, almost cursing at the team of horses that ran off. It was sort of funny to see this man of the cloth shaking his fists and yelling at these two spooked critters. To see such courage in letting his human side show in public was something you simply never saw from a reverend. Most that I ever saw and heard in church on Sundays, I felt they must be of a pious nature and up held the highest of standards so their flock might be led by a shepherd of great fortitude and morals. I think that this moment was exactly why I made friends with Pastor Thompson. He had the courage to be caught with his pants down, to be a human being. He became credible to me right then and there. It is then we became best friends,"

Jacob continued on with his point. "No, daughter, we have so much to do and so much to rebuild. Our days will be filled with hard work and meeting new friends to share our home. Then they will share the beauty of our memories. I reckon I have gone on for long enough now." Jacob said, and just kept walking with the willow stick tapping the oxen prodding them to keep going.

Katherine took her Father's hand and walked along with him all the rest of the way to Quincy.

Shortly after the wagons arrived, the laughter of children and a commotion of music and firecrackers was heard in a nearby clearing.

"Oh, Papa, may I go see?" Katherine asked.

Jakie jumped in and asked, "Please?"

Jacob looked up at Isobel sitting in the wagon seat. She smiled down on him and the children.

Jacob said, "All right, but you all be careful around those fireworks, and be back soon. Mr. Biggs is going to help us get camped on the other side of town. Don't get into any mischief, Jacob Junior, and mind your sister. You hear!"

The town of Quincy was celebrating a harvest like it had never experienced. It was a harvest jubilee and everyone was feasting and dancing and singing to music. Those musicians that were still with the train took their instruments and asked if they could join in and were welcomed with open arms.

Al sorts of things were happening. Lumberjack games were going on. The smell of fine pies of apple and berry and pumpkin was floating through the merriment, and after just staring at the sidelines, Isobel gave Jacob a gentle shove as he finally could not resist the drive to participate in the Lumbermen's games. He kissed Isobel and smiled a smile of great excitement. A smile that he had not expressed for over two thousand miles.

This was to be his celebration as well. The reason he came to California with all his dreams.

Chapter 45- Meeting the Feather

One! Two! Three! The gun sounded and eight teams of four men each gathered together for the start of the Lumbermen's games. The teams were to compete in all sorts of contests. Log rolling, tree felling, speed sawing, and trunk climbing. The winning team would get a 100-dollar prize to be divided among the four members equally. The first contest was the log cutting. Two men would take each handle of a bucksaw that was eight feet long with teeth as big as a tigers. The men spit on their hands and grabbed the ends of the saw. They placed it atop a log that was four feet thick, and braced for the starter gun to go off.

BANG! They were off and sawing. Back and forth: forth and back: as fast as they could go they sawed that log. And within a minute the first log cookie was cut and fell to the ground. The second two men of each team took up the saws and went to it, and another cookie fell, and another and another. Then it was Jacobs set to try with his teammate.

It was two months since he had a saw in his hands, but for him it was, well, like cutting logs. He grabbed that saw and he didn't lose any rhythm with it. It was as if he was a locomotive and was at as full head of steam. He did not even break a sweat.

Jacob was as at home as he had felt in a very long time. The smile that Isobel saw on his face was glowing with happiness.

The men on his team patted Jacob on his back. The handshakes came time after time, and Jacob's smile grew even bigger. He was lost in a world he had only dreamed of since they left Minnesota.

The next event was the climb. The men who climbed had to wear special boots with spikes and attached a strap of spurs to the back heels. They then wrapped themselves with a special strap that they then wrapped around the tree they were about to climb. The object to this event is to climb as fast as you can and when you get to the top ring a large bell, and then climb down as fast as you can, and then the next climber went up and did it all over again. The men could do the events as individuals, but this

was teamwork. Everything today was done in teams. Tomorrow the single man events would take place.

Today Jacob would be the anchorman for the climb: the last and most important position in this event. The fastest team would win.

The call went out to ready up for the event. The men got the gear set and strapped themselves up. Each pole was a tree that was topped and all the branches had been cut off. The tree was pretty much stripped of any obstacles that would get in the way of the straps. Each pole was topped to the height of one hundred feet, and each man had to climb all the way up to ring that bell.

ON YOUR MARK, GET SET. And the gun sounded the start.

They dug in and brought the straps up and up and up towards the tiptop to that bell. They would strap up and dig the spurs into the bark and move up bit by bit. It took all the strength they could muster. They used their legs, their arms, their backs, and most of all they had to use their wits. One false move or one slip of the strap and they could lose their very lives.

Jacob's turn was here. He wrapped the strap around the tree as if it was whip and securing the clip on the end to his harness, and with one leg up and then the other. To the top and the bell rung and like a clumsy rock Jacob went down the tree and just before the last ten feet he let go the strap and jumped the rest of the way. He had helped his team win another one.

Jacob was happy and tired all at the same time. Now they were about to undertake the most difficult contest of all the Lumbermen's games.

This was the Log Rolling.

Two men had to stand up on a log that was placed into the cold waters of the Feather River, gain their balance, and then roll the log in both directions trying to knock the other man off the log into the water. It was good way to have the opponent bathe if he hadn't for a time, and many lumberjacks needed one after being in the forest for days at a time.

The first two men stood their run and only one came out dry. The other was tossed aside into the cold waters, giving him the opportunity to take a bath and do his laundry at the same time. Then Jacob got his turn. This was not his favorite or his best event, but it was a great time to have good fellowship with others of his same occupation. There was no time to let your pride get in the way of having a good time.

Jacob got up; the other man did the same. The two men balanced themselves on the log and when the started called out the go, they proceeded to roll the log back and forth. The more they turned the wetter and more slippery the log became, and that made it harder to keep your balance. Only one could be left and soon with a splash and a holler, Jacob had met the Feather River waters.

Isobel and the children laughed as they witnessed their Jacob go into the water, somewhat disappointed, yet they could not help laughing. They knew he was a very happy man. Even if he was soaked to his bones through and through.

Chapter 46- Down the Feather River Road

The day ended with Jacob soaking wet, very tired and very happy. He stumbled out of the cold water and climbed to shore with the help of his new friends.

"Jacob, you roll a good log!" said Arne Knudsen one of his teammates. "You want to try again?" he laughed.

" No, I believe once in a day is quite enough for this man. I am sure my wife will appreciate the good bath I just had though. Perhaps we should teach the children how to roll a log?" Jacob said laughing right along with them all.

Isobel was standing nearby and heard every word.

"Jacob, you mind your tongue now. I do agree the children could use a good bath though. Maybe if we ..." Isobel got a sly and mischievous look about her face and called the children over to the bank of the river.

"Children, I want you to look at the sight your father has become."

Jacob knew what Isobel was up to and played along, so he put on the best shame filled face he could.

"He was having so much fun he near drowned himself in the river. He is soaked to the bones and his clothes are drenched. Now no argument here Jacob Summers you'll wake Emily. With all this commotion I am surprised she has not woken up."

Isobel directed Jacob to come to the edge of the river where they were standing.

"Husband what do you have to say for yourself?"

It was almost a crime to do what he was about to do, especially since Katherine spoke up in his defense.

"But, Mama, Papa was just having fun. Even he should some fun. After all the miles he has walked to get us here…"

Just as she began to give reason that he should not be scolded, Jacob lunged forward and managed to push each one, including Isobel, in to the icy cold of the Feather's waters.

With a scream and a giggle, they all surfaced from the dunking while Jacob was left standing on the bank laughing with his hands on his sides.

"Now, what do you think of a California bath, eh? It seemed to me you were all due."

Isobel looked at Jacob as if to say you are a dead man.

An indignant Isobel Summers holding her dress in her hands struggling to get out of the water got to the edge, managed to grab some grass on the bank. Just as the grass gave way, she fell back into the water.

This was too much for one woman to handle. What started to be a joke on the children had ended up with her being the brunt. Even the children could not help but laugh.

And, after a few seconds, even Isobel realized how hysterically funny the whole scene was and burst out with laughter as well. So she sat down right there in the water and like a child splashed about. The children and Jacob joined her and had the happiest time of their long journey together. Even Sam jumped in, and now the whole family was enjoying the cool water.

But, all good things must come to an end, and it was the same for the time in the water, though the bath felt refreshing, it was time to get back to business. They, after-all, were not to the end of the trail just yet. According to Mr. Biggs, there are about another hundred or so miles to go and it was going to be rough.

They had come through the plains lands of the Beckwourth Pass and now the trail would lead them over two gulches and down the currents of the Feather River itself.

But, how were they supposed to bring everything with them?

Katherine had no idea that this was going to be the most unusual way of transport they had ever experienced since the ferry crossing back in the Iowa territory.

"Papa? How are we going to get down river?" She asked. "The wagons are too big and we can't just leave the team?"

"I can answer that for you, young lady," Mr. Biggs piped up.

" We are going down the river just like all the rest have gone. We are going by wagon raft."

"What's that?" Jakie asked.

A wagon raft is a flatboat that we will each build. It will be big enough to hold not only the wagon, but your belongings as well," Mr. Biggs explained.

"But what about the teams? They won't stand for going on an open raft. What do we do with them?" Jacob asked.

"That is the hard part. Someone will have to take the teams and guide them along the side bank of the river," Mr. Biggs continued.

"This is slow, and sometimes you have to guide your team through some water."

"But, when the bank runs out and there is nothing to guide them along, what happens then?" Jacob asked. "I will have to be on the raft, but even if Jakie is the best to handle the team I don't want him doing this alone and far from us. There has got to be a better way."

Chapter 47- Fighting the Current

The questions began to fly at Mr. Biggs. What is the river like downstream? How much farther do we have? How deep is it? How is Jakie going to get that team past any obstacle he will encounter?

"Jacob, we cannot let our boy go it alone," Isobel begged.

"Most definitely *no* to Jakie is going down by himself," Jacob was firm on that decision.

"We could go Papa," Katherine said.

"NO! We will figure this out. But for right now, let us get some supper and think on this. If Mr. Biggs has any suggestions I for one will be listening," Jacob went back to the wagon to clean up.

The family went to get dried off and cleaned up from the dunking, and settled into a supper of cornbread and pork ribs with mashed potatoes and gravy that was being offered at the jubilee.

There was sour mash floating around in a special jug that one of the jacks brought to celebrate his winning all the contests. He was not so lucky... his foot was broken after a log cookie landed smack in the middle on top of his laces. It hit just so and snapped two bones clean in two. It was near the most dreadful scream anyone from those parts had ever heard, so that man pretty much drank the day away to ease the pain. He probably would not be his best ever again.

The night's celebrations were festive and colorful. The air was filled with music from two fiddlers and a string bass made from a washtub and a broomstick with only one string. There was an accordion, a guitar and a couple of Irish drums. All this made for a rhythmic evening. These folks didn't seem to ever be down in the mouth about anything, and everything was right with their world, at least this little piece of it.

As the night drew on, the eyes of the children got heavy with the weight of the days events. They were soon fast asleep.

"Good, now all the young ones are sleeping," Mr. Biggs quietly said. He continued.

"I wanted all the adults here to explain and answer your questions. I know you have never done anything

like a Wagon Raft before. It is going to take more work than you ever expected to do on the trail so far, but it has to be done. To rig the wagons and all your goods onto just one raft each will take the better part of a week. If we work together we can cut and build ten rafts and get them on their way by the end of the week. The rest will follow after the next few days," Mr. Biggs said.

"I vote we all go together," Mr. Simons said. "It will be safer and we can look out for each other. You know in case of Indian attack or more trail pirates."

"All in favor?" Mr. Biggs asked.

Everyone without hesitation said "Aye!"

"All right then we all go together," Then in the morning, have your best cutters and axes readied. We will have to cut around one hundred trees to build enough rafts for all the wagons, prepare them, build the rafts from those logs and then we have to unmount the wagons from their wheel and axle riggings. All your belongings that are not tied down will have to be secured. Anything loose will be lost along with the current. I'll bet you, it will be gone to the depths of the river bottom.

"Now, what about the teams and who leads them on the bank? I am not letting my son do it on his own. No sir, I am not!" Jacob was absolute in his feelings about the subject.

"No one said you would have to fend for yourselves in this. There are enough of us in the train left in this party that we can do this. Yes, guiding the teams on the bank will take time, but not as much time if you were to lose them in the river. The river has already taken many folks as well as their stock to watery end. We do this right, the way I tell you, or you stay here. Is that clear?" Mr. Biggs continued.

"The only way to get downstream together is to work together. No one family will have to guide their team by themselves. Each team will have two others along to help. We have just enough, but this is the way to do this. Three people on each raft. One for lookout and guidance on each front point and one to pole rudder the raft so it doesn't go too far a field.

Three folks guiding each team on the banks, one to harness, one to stick prod the team on each side to keep the animals moving. We need to cover several miles of river each day before we can rest. Not like on the trail where we could stop and rest at anytime. The river is not so forgiving. It is deep in parts and fast enough to take you with it if you are not careful.

So, get some sleep. The children have the right idea. I will see you at daybreak."

This new day was going to prove itself in many ways.

Chapter 48- Down the Feather

The new day began with the loud cracking of trees being felled and the humming and buzzing back and forth of huge bucksaws cutting through the timbers that were going to be built into the wagon rafts that would get the wagon train down the Feather.

Jacob was right at home with this cutting. He was glad to have his hands filled with an axe once again. He had almost forgotten what it felt like. His callouses were softening and he needed to toughen them up. It was a few months since they left the timber fields of Minnesota and it was too long a time since he had picked up an axe. He hadn't needed to. He was after all going to be on a trail to California with his family to find new fortune and make his fortune off the timber fields of their new home. What was he going to need an axe and saw for on the trail? Timber and sawdust chips were in his blood. He breathed them in and it gave him new life: a new energy to sustain him through each day. Tree sap ran through his veins and kept his heart pumping. Lumbering was in Jacob Summers. It was his life force and it was what made him the man he was. He was at home in the woods and was never happier than when he was lumbering, except for when he was with his family.

He had done other things to make a living as a young man but trees… oh trees were the root of his very soul. Jacob knew how to grow them, harvest them, and conserve groves that would benefit from alternate cutting times. He was probably the best lumberman, other than Mr. Big John MacKaskill himself, Minnesota ever knew.

The men of the train weren't all as experienced as Jacob. They had come to depend upon his knowledge of what tree to fall and how to make it fall where it would not kill anyone when it hit the ground or shatter into pieces when it met mother earth.

The loud alert of "TIMBER" was being called as one after another fell to earth with a great crash. Men surrounded each tree and began to saw the trees into shorter lengths. Each log was hand hewn into the logs that were to be used for the wagon raft beams.

Much of the bark from each tree was left on to help shed water, and to help keep a steady tread for footing. Rope made from sisal plants was prepared to tie the logs together. Special wood pegs were made by the carpenters to pin the log rafts together, with the ropes securely holding as an extra rigging the rafts had a better chance of surviving being bashed about the boulders that lined the riverbanks.

Pounding, chopping, sawing, hammering, an occasional curse word for smashed fingers sake , could be heard all over the compound.

"Hey, Jacob!" Oli Swenson asked, "How are we going to get these crafts into the water after we build them? We still have to take the wagons off their wheels and put them on board each of these. This is going to take more time than we thought, I think."

Jacob dropped his axe where he stood and walked to the riverbank. He scratched his head and a puzzled look appeared on his face.

"Humm. That might just work," Jacob said out loud. "Mr. Biggs how did they do it before we came round?" Jacob asked.

Mr Biggs answered, "Well, let's see. Some used block and tackle to hoist each raft with a wagon on it into the water, but I don't see any trees that look like they could handle the weight. These wagons aren't light by any means. They carry some hefty pounds with all your folks belongings."

Just then, Jacob noticed a few of the children playing with some sticks lined up next to each other side by side. On top of the sticks was large rock that they were gently pushing back and forth with simplistic ease.

It passed the time for them and it was great play.

"What are you children doing?" Jacob asked.

"Papa, we are playing as if this rock is a wagon going to California. We don't have any wheels so we used these sticks to roll the rock back and forth. We learned about this in school," Jakie said. "Our teacher said this is what they did to move parts for big buildings."

"Son, you may have just saved us all a whole lot of struggle. Mr. Biggs we have a solution!" Jacob ran off to tell the others of the plan.

Trees of a similar size and roundness were cut to even out the rolling motion and to make it easier to transport a loaded raft to the waters edge.

"All right, but how do we get the wagon rafts to water?" Oli asked.

"That's simple. We build each raft on the rollers. We will take out the belongings, take off the wheels from each wagon and lay them down. With our own strength we will lift the wagon onto the wheels, and then put the belongings back into the wagons. Then to get the rafts into the water we will lever the rollers forward to push it over a sloped bank that we will make. Each craft should gently slide into the river. It sounds easy enough. Tomorrow we'll know for sure."

Chapter 49-
The Watery Trail

"**H**eave Ho! Heave Ho! Alright one more time should do it," you could hear the men say as they lifted each wagon onto the wagon raft supports.

"These sure are heavy; heavier than I have ever lifted before even without our goods in them," said Mr. Brannigan.

The wheels were taken off each wagon, placed on the raft riggings and at each corner. The wagon was brought down and laid across them. The wheels acted like bumpers and would help deflect the big rocks and bushes as the wagon raft went down the river. They would help keep the wagon safe from bashing against the huge boulders that lay hidden just below the water.

Chapter 49- The Watery Trail

"Now, the hard part," Jacob said. "We have to put the belongings back in each wagon,"

Before each wagon could be hoisted, all the belongings including the foodstuffs and teams had to be removed. Every cover, every cover ribbing, everything came off. The wagon was lifted by the block and tackle that were used at the lumber camp nearby. The men of the camp helped out - and a good thing too. Without them, it would be just about impossible for the men of the train to lift every wagon in good time. A schedule had to be met and it is was up to the men to keep it.

Autumn was close behind and, with it, would be the first snows. The snows would bring the first melt and the river would begin an early crest making it unsafe for travel.

It took hours for each wagon to be unloaded, get it rigged for hoisting, and then the men had to physically lever it into the water with the help of the log rollers. The raft would be steered by three people. One in the back to act as a tiller man, the other two would be towards the front with long poles to help guide the raft and keep it away from any rocks or hazards that might show perilous. That was not an easy job to have.

It took the better part of a week to get all the remaining wagons emptied and started down the Feather River to better digs. The wagons got jarred and continually bumped into the riverbank to begin. The wagons had been piloted by people who had

Chapter 49 - The Watery Trail

no idea what it meant to be sailors, much less just passengers on a flat raft made of simple logs.

The rafts measured 25 feet long and at least half as wide. The water clearance was nil and the water was always splashing on the deck. It was a wet journey for those who had many belongings. Those with not as many, did not have the big worry of drying out their belongings at the end. The wagons were tied to shore trees before they were let go down the river.

"Mr. Biggs are you going to follow on shore and help those who may need it?" one man asked.

"Yes, I will be right behind the teams with my horse and riggings in case there is need. It will be slow, but, it will be a sure trail. I have done the riverbank trail before, never done the raft. I am not sure I would do well with that. I think I will stick to dry earth. Something about having my two feet on solid ground makes me feel more at ease. 'Sides the only water I prefer to be associated with is the type I can either take a good long bath in or the type I can drink a good long drink of. I'll see you folks down river. There is a spot there that is perfect to hitch for the night.

You'll get there before we do so get to that spot and tie down securely so we have no more disasters. We will be along directly. Remember once you get on the water stay to the middle, and when the rapids…"

Brannigan piped up, "Rapids what rapids? I thought this would be a smooth river.

Nobody said anything about rapids."

Jacob said, "Every river has rapids. You just grab

the wagon, hold on, and hope for the best. Oh ! And don't lose the guide poles. We lose our guide poles we have no way to steer. So take care in stowing them. Remember that. You are steering one of the wagons as tiller man."

"I can't do that!" Mr. Brannigan said. "I would just as soon stay here on dry land than to risk life and limb in a river that has rapids. You know, I may just do that."

"Well, make your mind up. I suppose we'll help get your things back on land if you choose so. Your rig and team is already headed up river and it will take several days to get them back. What's it going to be?" Jacob reminded.

The men stared with arms crossed waiting for a reply and a decision.

Chapter 49 - The Watery Trail

Chapter 50-
Terror in the Canyon

Mr. Brannigan stood there looking into the eyes of each man who had used sweat and strength to load and launch his wagon down the river.

"Well what's it going to be Brannigan? You made up your mind yet?" One man asked.

Jacob said, "Nathan you have come this far. As far as any of us. You have braved rainstorms, dust storms, and bees when the girls got into trouble. You were there when the mountain lion attacked us in the desert, and now you don't want to go because of some rapids? I don't know about you; but I tell you, after all that, there is nothing going to stop me from getting to our new home. Going down rapids, I imagine isn't going to be as easy as cutting into a piece of pie. Maybe a little messy but in the end it will be so smooth and nice that it will seem like an cool evening in the rocker on the front porch drinking a lemonade.

Just remember, your things are already on the raft and in the river. You have to get them if you are thinking of staying here. You will be doing that on your own I am sure. No one here wants to go backwards on the trail when they are so close to being at the end of it."

"You always speak sense Jacob Summers. I have always admired that about you. You are right. I will come with you all and help pilot the rafts, ... even if I cannot swim," Mr. Brannigan said.

"What? You can't swim! I thought everybody knew how to swim at least the dog paddle. That should be no worry. I've been told by locals the river is not up. The mountain snows have not begun to fall and the new early melt is not due for several weeks. You saw how well we built the rafts; you helped build them for Pete's sake. Are you still afraid of a bit of water?" Jacob asked.

Mr. Brannigan hung his head in embarrassment for not knowing how to swim.

"I tell you what, you come with me and together we will pilot your raft down river. How would that be?" Jacob suggested.

"Like I said you always seem to speak sense Jacob," Mr. Brannigan said.

The two men helped launch the last two rafts into the

Feather River and tied them to a tree along the bank.

"Isobel you, Jakie and the girls head down the bank. It should be easy. The trail is well marked, just keep watch of difficulties. Jacob Jr. you help keep watch. Do what you can son.

Girls you help your mother with Emily. To keep up, your little sister will need to be carried for most of the trail. Don't forget Mr. Biggs is not far off. He will be in shouting distance if you need anything. Go slow and steady. We don't know what to expect in this canyon. I will see you all soon," Jacob slapped the oxen team on the haunches and in the way that only oxen can, they gave a slight jerk and in a slow but steady gait, they got going.

The last rafts and their passengers launched off down the river with the citizens of the lumber camp waving them all a hearty goodbye and Gods speed for a safe journey.

With a loud, "Thank you," the remainder of the Summers Wagon Train was on their way.

"Alright now, keep your rifles handy. You have your canteen nearby? Keep a good grip on the guide poles now and keep watch above us. No telling what is up there. Mr. Biggs said to still keep a look out for the trail pirates. He said some might be lurking along the canyon trails above us," Jacob cautioned.

The river was smooth as glass. It held an occasional bump from underneath the surface but nothing to be too concerned about. Each man at each point poled the raft carefully and with what became a skill they did not know they had in them. The canyon of the Feather was quiet and still. Almost a strange eerie quiet. A quiet that made the men become suspicious of the silence. It looked like it would last for miles along the watery trail. But up ahead a sight for sore eyes was spotted. The first teams from the train were seen trodding along the riverbank.

A HELLO was called from the rafts. Everyone along the banks stopped to wave and say "ARE YOU ALL RIGHT? ANY PROBLEMS?"

"NO, NO PROBLEMS. SEE YOU ALL UP AHEAD. WE KNOW WHERE TO STOP FOR THE NIGHT. WE WILL MEET YOU THERE."

And the rafts continued onward down the river.

But, there it was again. That silent spookiness, like the rock walls were talking to them. They creaked and cracked with small pieces of gravel tumbling off the canyon walls. They were coming down splashing into the water. This was not unusual, so the men did not think too much of it, but there it was again only this time it was louder Then a more violent CRACK! It echoed down the canyon as if a willowthewisp was let loose. An entire wall of canyon boulders and gravel came falling into the water like so many stars falling from the sky. Boulders, stones and finally one of the walls came down into the water causing the rafts to sway and rock. The men were hanging on for life itself and trying their best to keep the raft, that was being rocked back and forth, from being destroyed. They held the guide poles and held on for their lives.

Then it happened, the largest boulder just teetering from atop the canyon came plummeting downward right towards Nathan's raft.

"PUSH! PUSH HARD! PUSH QUICKLY! OH, NO! JUMP!"

Chapter 51- One More Day

CRASH! A large boulder dropped out of the sky. It hit the middle of the raft as if it were shot from a sharp shooters rifle. Dead on, it hit the center of the wagon, the raft and all the belongings.

What happened to the men? They all dived into the river, but none of them surfaced from the Feather's icy current.

The raft was in splinters. Pieces of logs were floating and bobbing down the river. The wagon was nowhere to be seen. A chest of drawers and a small cupboard were drifting along in the ripples of the remnant of the wave where the boulder entered the water.

The men piloting the rafts ahead of Nathan's saw what happened and as quickly as they could gain control of their rafts poled them to the bank and secured them to some rocks on shore. They tried to help. They ran up the bank to the sight of the crash and searched for any sign of the men who were on board. One man dove into the water and swam down into the depths of the cold river.

"LOOK! There! Over there on the cupboard! I see one!"

On one of the cupboards, Mr. Brannigan had managed to climb on to save himself from drowning. He was draped across the lower front leg just hanging on. He had been thrown from the raft and swept up into the currents wave when the boulder hit. It threw him farther down river where the cupboard was floating nearby. He managed to gather all his strength and pull himself onto the piece of kitchen furniture. He looked like he was about unconscious, but it was easy to tell he was breathing.

"Take this rope and swim out to tie it onto the cupboard and we'll pull it back to shore."

One man swam out as fast as his arms would go. He caught up and tied the rope to the furniture and to Mr. Brannigan so he would not fall back into the water.

Time was short and the men knew they must get Brannigan onto dry land. He would either die of exposure or he would fall back into the water and die for sure. These men were his only chance of surviving.

But what of Jacob and the other man? They were nowhere to be seen.

"Quickly, go and search the riverbank where it happened. See what you can find."

Two men looked for Jacob Summers and Ethan Emry. It was as if they were taken by God himself straight to heaven. Just snatched from this earth.

That quiet eeriness returned to the canyon walls. A silence even quieter than before.

"Wait. Did you hear that?" One man asked. "Be quiet maybe we'll hear it again."

"Cough! Cough!" It was coming from on top of some rocks on the other side. The men stopped and looked and listened as sharply as they could to locate where the sound was coming from.

"Over there on those boulders where the gravel shoal is. That is Ethan Emry."

One man swam over and revived Ethan.

" Are you going to be all right my friend? What happened to Jacob, did you see him?"

Between coughing and choking up water, Ethan Emry told what happened to Jacob before they all jumped from getting hit.

"Jacob pushed Brannigan into the water and then me. He was still on the raft when it was smashed. I did not see what happened afterwards. All I remember is that I went under and blacked out until I woke up with you helping me. I reckon the water wave brought me up here to this here rock. I am a bit bruised and beaten but I think I will be all right.

I don't know what happened to Brannigan or Jacob," he said in a daze.

"We have Brannigan, but we have seen no sign of Jacob."

From across the river they called out. "IS IT ETHAN?

"YES HE WILL BE ALRIGHT."

"ANY SIGN OF JACOB?"

"NO! NOT OVER HERE! YOU KEEP LOOKING! I WILL GET ETHAN. CALL OUT IF YOU FIND JACOB."

The men were running up and down the riverbank trying with all there might to locate Jacob Summers. Where could the man be? They started to speculate and guess if he might have drowned or was washed up on shore or maybe he got caught in the under current of the river, or maybe he was caught by he boulders force and was sunk with the huge rock.

The men went farther up the bank and back down again at least a dozen times, and still nothing.

Shortly after, the familiar sound of bells on oxen was coming up the bank and the sight of folks coming down with the arriving teams.

"Oh, no! Isobel is going to want to know if Jacob is all right. What are we going to tell her and the children?"

"We tell her the truth."

Chapter 52- The Search for Jacob Summers

"The folks with the teams will be showing up pretty soon. I already see some coming up the bank," Oli said.

A few miners who were camped nearby came to help when they heard the commotion.

"What's happening here?" one of them asked.

"We have a man in the river and we cannot find him. We can use the extra hands if you'd be willing."

Everyman set his hands and feet to searching the banks some more.

"Anything over there?" they shouted.

"I don't see nothing!" came the answer.

A group of men were standing on the bank scanning the opposite side of the river.

Suddenly a shout… "LOOK OVER THERE IN THAT CREVICE! THE ONE WITH THE LOG STICKIN UP. IS THAT HIM? ALL I CAN SEE IS AN ARM. BUT, IT MIGHT BE HIM!"

On the other side of the river was a flowing inlet. In that inlet were some small shallow caves and in one of those caves strung over a log, teetering on a boulder, was Jacob Summers. He was lifeless and did not move a muscle. It looked like he was dead.

"GO GET HIM. TAKE THIS ROPE AND WE WILL HELP PULL HIM BACK. KEEP HIS HEAD UP OUT OF THE WATER."

Two men swam across the river and tied Jacob with the rope. They both jumped in and then pulled Jacob in behind them holding his head above the water.

"PULL, MEN! PULL!"

"There has been many a time that Jacob Summers helped us. Just look at all the times he helped each one of us get across the prairie. No, not now, Jacob Summers! You are not going to die today my friend!" Oli said.

Each man grunted and pulled with all their strength against the current of the Feather.

Soon, the men and Jacob were close enough to shore that they could get Jacob standing and with help from the others, he was brought on shore.

"Careful don't lose him! Don't bump his head now. Lay him down here."

"Turn him on his stomach and push on his back. That should get any water out of him." One miner told them.

Jacob lay still on the water soaked gravely bank. His face was turned into the sand and his arms lay quiet.

"The teams are getting closer. I see Isobel and the children coming!"

"We can't let her see Jacob like this. Not after what they have been through." Oli said.

As soon as that was said Jacob inhaled a deep water filled breath and coughed up water and whatever else it might have been that he swallowed in the river.

He gave a few more deep hacking coughs and sat up on his own.

"Did I hear you say Isobel was coming with the teams? Never in my life did I ever let that woman see me injured and I am not to start now. Get me off this sand, and stand me up. I'll be alright," Jacob said.

He voiced all the grunts and groans he could, just to stand. He rubbed his head and found a large spot of blood on the back of his head. His hand was bloodied by the gash. He quickly knelt down and washed himself off as if nothing at all had happened.

He brushed himself off as best he could and did what he could to help the men with Mr. Brannigan and Ethan Emry. They were not in the best of shape either and it showed.

Soon the teams began to arrive at the site of the accident.

"My lord what happened here!?" Ethan's wife asked.

"Rock avalanche. We got hit pretty bad by some big boulders off the canyon face.

They came straight down and destroyed our raft. We ain't even begun to look for the belongings," Ethan said.

With more teams arriving and the noise of the ruckus up ahead Katherine ran to see what the problem was.

She instantly saw her Father soaked to the bone and a wagon raft in a thousand splinters along side the waters edge.

"What happened here?"

Chapter 53- On Dry Land

Katherine saw blood on her father's shoulder that was dripping from his head.

"Papa, you're bleeding!" Frightened, Katherine ran back to her Mother.

"Momma, Papa is hurt bad, come quick!"

Isobel quickly gave the reins to Jake and told him to look after Emily. Isobel ran the rest of the way with Katherine to see how bad off Jacob was.

"Jacob, Jacob, Katherine said your are hurt bad. What happened? Are you all right? Where are you hurt?" Isobel asked.

"Your daughter gets riled easy. I am fine. Just a bit wet and I did get hit on the head with a rock or two.

No broken bones. No missing limbs. See I even still got all my teeth. I am okay woman. I could use some doctoring on my head I reckon," Jacob said trying to reassure Isobel.

Now it could not be missed. The blood was dripping downward off Jacob's head like he had just come in from a rainstorm.

Isobel's eyes grew like teacup saucers.

"You sit down here on this dry sand Jacob Summers. I will tell you who is in need of doctoring. You hard headed old fool; you can't keep your injuries secret from me. I know when you been hurt, I always have. Like the time you came in from mending the fence on the corral. You walked into the house with your hand slung in your suspenders. You said, "That's enough for the day," but I could tell you hit your fingers with the hammer just by looking at the swelling and black and blue color your hand took on. I know you better than you know. So hold still and let me stitch this head of yours."

Jacob sat and held his breath while Isobel sewed up the gash in the back of his scalp. With every poke of the sewing needle Jacob let go a loud "Ouch!" along with a wince of his shoulders.

"Will you watch what you are doing!"

Isobel said, "That is why I am almost done."

She put the needle and thread back in the sewing pouch and said, "That wasn't so bad now was it? You sit right here and rest. From the looks of your reddish hair you lost quite a bit of blood.

SO STAY PUT or you will not hear the end of it!"

Katherine was watching every stitch her mother made. She giggled a little under her hand when she heard her father being told to behave.

Jacob saw his eldest daughter smirk and smile at his infirm situation and he shook his finger at Katherine. "Young lady you mind yourself now, you hear. Now help your brother get the team."

While Jacob sat as he was told Isobel helped the others get Mr. Brannigan and Ethan doctored as well.

Both were conscious and soaked down to their skin, but they were very thankfully alive and doing all right considering what they had been through. "Get blankets! Someone get some coffee going. We could all use it," Isobel said.

The three men sat together on the sandy shore shivering and blaming away about how the river was going to be smooth sailing and nothing dangerous was going to happen.

"Jacob Summers I blame you for this mess. I come all this way to end up with nothing. All my belongings are at the bottom of this confounded river. My wagon, my furniture, even my poke to buy the new homestead was in the wagon."

Jacob replied, "No it's not. When I saw the rock going to crash down upon us, I snatched up your valuables bag and then jumped into the river. Do you know how heavy that bag is? It almost nearly drowned me. What do you have in that bag anyway?"

Mr. Brannigan noticed it wasn't on shore with them.

"Alright then where is it if you saved the bag?"

They all looked around, and then a water soaked, yet, bright paisley bag sat waiting on the top of that log that Jacob was retrieved from. It was still sitting atop that log most comfortably in that quiet eddy in the cave not having budged one inch.

"Well alright go get it Jacob," Brannigan said most matter of factly.

Jacob simply replied, "I saved it once, so it is your turn to get your belongings. Besides I was told to sit here until further orders."

Jacob crossed his arms in stubborn rebellion and held his ground. It was the easiest excuse he ever could have come up with.

"I must remember to thank Isobel for telling me to sit here," he thought.

"I am staying here on dry land. That bag is much too heavy for one man to attempt to carry cross river. It weighs like a lead brick. It would drown you for sure Mr. Brannigan. You wait right here with the two of us and we will get some help later. Your poke isn't gone, it's just delayed.

Chapter 54- The Miners

There they were, sitting side by side, the three men who, after being rained down upon with gravel and rocks as if sent from heaven, and after surviving the ultimate insult of being targeted by the largest boulder God could ever have thought of, sat on the gravelly sandy beach draped with blankets, drenched to their inner being: each drinking their fair share of the coffee provided. Sitting there like the three monkeys from hear, see, and speak no evil.

All they managed to do was complain at each other and place blame on one another, one with more blame than the next, shivering cold with their fair share of hurts and scrapes at the same time, and gabbing about.

Each comparing how bad the injuries were from being bombed by pieces of the canyon walls. Every injury became more severe than the previous. At least they made it sound that way.

Isobel and the rest just about thought the three would turn to stone if anyone of them admitted to any wrong doing at all. Heaven forbid they have anything to do with anything wrong. After all they were men and being men should uphold all that was true and strong and ….

"All right you three, time to get up and help the rest of us," Isobel said. "Jacob are you well enough to get up without falling down? Let me see your head. Yes, that will heal just fine. These stitches look a little red but they will clean up just fine. No one will even know you got hurt after the hair grows back. You are going to have a headache for a while but it will probably not hurt that bad, being as hard headed as you are. Do you understand what I am saying here Jacob Summers?"

Isobel faced her husband and sternly looked at him then turned away to get the nights bedding ready for the children.

Tomorrow was going to another day and Mr. Brannigan's poke bag was not going anywhere. No fool would even try to get the bag by himself.

The night disappeared in the dew of the new morning. The smell of the breakfast seemed more delicious for some reason, nothing extra special about the ingredients this time. It was the same thing they have had for many days, almost to the point of being boring. So boring in fact the taste buds of everyone in camp were about to leave their tongues behind for new territory.

"Mama. I do love your breakfasts. They always smell so good," Katherine said.

Jakie up with a stretch and a wide yawn."Morning mama. What's for breakfast?"

"We have some eggs we got on the trail. One of the miners wives traded us for some things she needed. By the way, where is Katey? Find her please, and tell her breakfast's almost ready."

Katey was already up and gone to the river bank to watch the men retrieve Mr. Brannigan's valuables from the other side of the river. This was going to prove interesting.

"All right one of you is going to get wet. It is just a matter of deciding which of you it is to be." Brannigan said.

"You had better appreciate this Brannigan. After all the trouble you have caused for some of us and now you are giving commands and telling us what to do. Why I have half a mind to…" One of the men said.

His comment was interrupted by the sight of Gridley Biggs on his horse coming up the trail riding proudly with a parade of miners following with all sorts of tools and block and tackle. All to help with the retrieval of Mr. Brannigan's valuables bag and even what they could save from the Feathers' freezing waters at the bottom.

Following Mr. Biggs, was a line of miners that numbered some 50 plus. All sorts: big ones, little miners, miners from other countries, but all of them carrying something to help this small band of pioneers get whatever was left of their life and belongings.

They began by getting a rope from one bank to the other, and equipped with block and tackle they rigged the ropes with a sort of free swinging trolley so they could bring things back and forth between each bank. The first thing they retrieved was Mr. Brannigan's precious valuables bag with his poke still inside. A lot wetter that before, but still there just the same.

The next thing the miners were rigging was something that only a lumberman would have known. It was triangular in shape and had so many ropes hanging off its frame it looked like some sort of sea monster. But this was going to prove itself the most remarkable piece of engineering anyone of the pioneers had ever seen.

Chapter 55- Raising the Wagon

This contraption was one of the most unusual frames anyone ever saw. Ropes and all sorts of block and tackle riggings were coming off the monster triangular frame. It reached out over the river with a giant arm and looked like it could just grab up anything it came in contact with. It was two huge fir triangular frames, about twenty feet across at the bottom. One triangle frame had to be pulled to the other side and braced up. Then the large rough sawn beam that went across the two frames had to be set across the top so it would reach to each bank. The beam itself was about forty feet across, and about twelve inches square. It needed to be, so the block and tackle could be rigged and would hold everything it was supposed to. It took the better part of a day to build it. Lucky for them they had the trees nearby that could be used to build it with, and more so, the men who could build it.

The more ropes and riggings that were put on it, the more it looked like it would indeed work. But, would it?

In order for it to succeed, someone had to have guts enough to dive back into the river pulling a thin rope so's not to weigh them down too much, go to the very bottom of the wreckage and pull the trailing ropes under and over almost the entire wagon or at least what was left of it.

The frame was up and the ropes and pulleys were set and daylight was burning away into the early evening.

"All right, who's going to do the deed? That water is cold and it is swift down below. Someone has to be able to hold their breath for a long time and haul those ropes over and under all sorts of angles and then tie them so the men on shore can haul it up out from the watery tomb," one miner instructed.

The instant the man finished talking, two petite women, both dressed in a sort of white pajama wrapped round them, stepped from the crowd. They placed on to their faces some strange sort of glasses. Their way of speaking was different, too.

"We will do it. We will place the ropes. We can do it. Where do you want them to be?"

They both smiled. Their names were Yoshei and Ketsuko.

"We are from Nippon. We can do this job."

The men laughed and chuckled, "You two little ladies better just step back now and let someone who has some strength in their arms take over." Mr. Brannigan said. "Where did they come from anyhow?"

One miner spoke up, "I bought them, actually sort of rented them you might say, because of a special skill they have. You ever been to Nippon mister? Well, if you had, you would know that these here ladies are the most skilled divers in the world. They fish for oysters and other shellfish by diving into the ocean waters with knives and small buckets to gather the shellfish at the sea bottom. They can haul up their own weight in fish and shellfish, and best of all they can hold their breath for a very long time. They can hold their own, don't you worry about them. 'Sides, how are you going to tie the ropes to the sunken wagon?"

"Why are they here with you?" Brannigan asked.

"I use them to help me mine for gold in the river. Because they can hold their breath for so long they help me find nuggets at the bottom of the river. Pretty good at it. They bring up a good bit too.

They wanted to come to America and this is how they are paying for their trip. Pretty soon, they will have paid me in full. These ladies are making me rich. You can bet your bottom dollar on them. They will get it done."

Amazed, Brannigan said "Now, I have seen everything. Well ladies let's see what you can do."

Yoshei and Ketsuko took the ropes in hand and prepared their breathing for a long stint under the water. Finally, with a splash they dove in and, like two fish, went straight for the bottom.

"They must have found something; the ropes are moving up here."

Everyone stopped and stared in amazement. Ropes would go and then stop and then go again. Then more rope would be hauled out. In just a few seconds the divers came to the surface with each one holding two gold nuggets to help pay their debt.

Ketsuko said, "The ropes are ready. You may pull the wagon up now."

Ten men gathered around the block and tackle rigging and each one rubbed their hands, cracked their knuckles and some even spit on their hands to give a better grip to the ropes.

One man called out, "All right now, take up the slack and let's get this mans life to the surface!"

The ropes went taught the second the men started pulling. The ropes and riggings began to squeak and creak. The framing was creaking as well and the masting at the front of the frame was beginning to bow towards the ground from the weight of the wagon and the pressure of the water. It was heavier than they had all anticipated.

"More men! We need more men!"

Eight more grabbed a'hold and with all their strength pulled and grunted. The frame creaked louder and one of the rope riggings began to unravel at the top.

"Come on men. We can do it! Just a little more! A little more! Come on now! Give one good heave!"

With that said the wagon broke the surface of the water. There wasn't much to look at. The cover was gone and the metal ribs were bent and one side was completely destroyed, but it looked like it was a wagon at one time and could probably be repaired. There it swung in mid air with water draining from both sides. After a time and with the water drained away it made the wagon much easier to haul in.

"Wait! What about my wheels! I cannot go anywhere without my wheels," Brannigan said.

Yoshei grabbed another rope and dove back in. In no time she had all four wheels roped and tied to come to shore, and when she surfaced once more she held two more nuggets in her hand "Well, it looks like Mr. Brannigan and his wagon has done us a world of good. It looks like you have helped us find a strike. I wish you well on your journey, sir. We have to get back to work," the miner said.

The ladies dove back in while the miner stood there with two other armed men with shotguns slung across their arms, standing next to him. It wasn't so nobody would steal the gold; it was so no one would kidnap the divers.

Chapter 56- Fifty Miles About

"Well it looks like I am hoofin it for a time. At least, I still have my poke stake and my team. I am no worse for the wear and it is only a short more distance to Bidwell Bar. Mr. Biggs said it was only 50 miles about. If I can trek across country on foot, be attacked by a big cat and get rained on by giant boulders and almost lose my life, I can walk fifty miles," Mr Brannigan said.

Mr. Brannigan had a different tone to his attitude and demeanor. The man sounded to have almost given up. He was quieter and more humble. He didn't even give anyone an argument about anything.

He just took the reins of his team and willowed the oxen's haunches and continued on down the riverbank with the rest of who were following the river bank.

Katherine asked her mother, "Mama, is Mr. Brannigan all right? He looks sad."

Isobel answered, "He has just been through more than any man should have to endure. He and your Father and Ethan have just gone through what we call "the mill of life" and come out on the other side still alive, barely, but still breathing. He'll be all right."

"What about Papa? He'll be all right too won't he?" Jakie asked.

" Yes, in all his hard headedness he will be fine. He will walk for a while with a limp in his leg and lump on his head but he will be just fine. We must help him for a few days. He will tire easily and …"

"LOOK MAMA! There's our wagon!" Jakie shouted.

The wagon raft was moored on the river bank just a short run from the trail.

The children hurried over to see if everything was all right. Isobel and Jacob went to see for themselves if everything was still together.

"It looks to be in good shape. Wheels are still intact and the raft is safe. Yep everything looks fine. I guess we *are* fortunate. Have been all the way here. With only the croup to hold us up when your sister became sickly, you could say we have an angel watching our every step," Jacob said.

"I am so glad the wagon is still together," Isobel said.

"Why Mama? What is so important that wagon is still together?" Katherine asked.

"Because, daughter, that is where we are going to live until your father gets our new home built."

"You mean we all have to sleep together in the wagon? Even Jakie? It won't hold all of us," Katherine said.

" Yes it will, because Jakie and your Father will be sleeping outside and all the ladies of the family will sleep in the comfort of our mattress inside the wagon. You can do anything. You and Katey survived bee stings and hot sun across the desert. You even survived the big rainstorm back in the Iowa territory. You young lady, are a Summers and we come from firm and sturdy stock. If you are not toughened by now I would wonder about you," Isobel said.

The trail just kept winding along the river bends. It drifted along side the waters edge a few times and was even lost to some places where the water covered the trail.

"Jacob you take Emily. I will make sure the children ride on the team to clear the water. This one is pretty deep." Isobel helped each of the children climb aboard the oxen to stay head clear of the water to get to the other side. It was only a few feet deep, but it was enough to be cautious about. As they all realized, the river could change course in an instant and they could all be washed away oxen and all.

Crossing the river in the small eddy was an easy time.

They came across a little colder and much wetter than they had started but they could continue on.

"There is only about a mile or two left before we stop for the night. The rafts will meet us all down to the camp sight. I told the men to start fires and get things going so we can all dry out. One man said he could catch some fresh fish for supper and we can have fresh meat once again. Don't lose heart now folks. We are so close you can feel the soft breeze gently float over the trees. Like a mamas touch to her little ones cheek isn't it?" Mr Biggs said.

The Wagon Master described it like it was a soft and whispered lullaby. A feeling that we could all simply float on, into a dreamy sleep and then when we waked up we would be at our new home. The time over the next few days, would prove to be most valuable to us all as a family and as a wagon train.

Chapter 57-
Mud and Blood and Too Much Good Times

The day drew on along the well-traveled riverbank. The dusty wheel rutted road showed the memories of the many pioneers who went before to gain their fortune and new home. The canyon walls seemed to be climbing higher alongside, and if you listened real close you could almost hear your heartbeat echo in the silence of the trail.

Each team was steadily walking along the trail and each team guide would occasionally have to give them a touch of the willow whip to keep them on an even path. At least they did not need to search for water or green grass to feed them. The teams were much calmer.

"Mama, what do you think it will be like? Our new home, I mean," Katherine asked.

"You asked me this before didn't you?" Isobel answered.

"I know but I enjoy hearing it."

"Well let's see. Why don't you ask Mr. Biggs? He knows this place we are headed better than any one of us. He'll be the one that can tell you."

Isobel's suggestion caught Katherine's young mind and she lit up like a newly started campfire.

"May I go, Mama? I want to go ask Mr. Biggs like you said. I won't be long."

"All right child, you run along and take Katey. She hasn't had anytime away from your little sister for a spell. Katey you go ahead. I'll mind Emily."

Jakie piped up, "Me too Mama?"

"Not this time. Your father is not well enough yet to handle the oxen, I need you to help with the team while I hold Emily. You two don't be long and mind your step now. We don't want to be fishing you out of the river."

The girls ran off as Isobel was reminding them to be careful.

"They are truly your children Jacob Summers. Even Katey reminds me of you."

Isobel walked closely to her husband and gently took his hand with affection and smiled at him.

"When do you think we will be there, Jacob?" Isobel asked.

"Well, from what Mr. Biggs said, we will be to the

destination in just a few days. He said that there is a spot on the trail where the trail splits off and goes south for a time, but we want to head straight on towards Bidwell Bar. We are only going to stay there long enough to sneeze and gather some supplies. He said don't expect much. It is a pretty rowdy place. He told me the miners there have been away from their homes for many months and they have they have lost the kindness of civilization and the courtesy of the manners they were brought up with. There will be lots of mud, and fist fights at the saloons. He said there are many as ten saloons in that settlement, which only gave way to, too much good times and not enough temperance.

Our new home isn't far after that. He said two days at most. Our new home is supposed to have forests and greenery in such abundance we will have no worries. It has decent farmland to grow whatever we want and weather so good it would make you wonder if winter ever comes."

"Do you think we might have a porch again? I did so enjoy the evenings in the cool air rocking?" Isobel asked.

"Yes I will be sure to build our house bigger than the last. It will be built from fresh timbers. Hewned from the strongest trees, and built with such great skill it will never fall away into the dust. It will last almost forever! Do you think that will do you, wife?"

"Isobel just held Jacob's hand a little more firmly and continued on. She just smiled and didn't need to

say a word. They had made the trip and were almost finished and closer to the dream Jacob had so many weeks ago.

Soon Katherine and Katey came running back to help their parents.

"You're back so quickly? You didn't make pests of yourselves now did you?" Jacob asked.

Katey explained Mr. Biggs needed to ride ahead and ready a camp ground for the evening and make sure everything was safe and sound. He was going to help the remaining rafts secure for the night.

Night fell fast. Where they camped was tree lined and filled with the fresh smell of burning logs on the fire. The dinner in the cast iron pans was simmering with the cuttings of filleted fresh fish caught from the Feather. The air was calm with just a slight breeze flowing through the campground. It was truly peaceful.

The citizens of the train were all gathered round the fire.

"What now Mr. Biggs? We have a days ride into Bidwell Bar and then that is where we all part company. I heard there is good work on the north ridge up to a place called Sterling City. Supposed to be good harvest up there. Trees as big as houses, I heard," one man said.

"I heard the land in the valley below was rich and fertile. Enough for everyone who wanted to farm," Ethan Emry added.

"Don't forget the mining. That's what I came for.

I am bound and determined to make my fortune come flood or famine, and I am not returning without anything in this pouch. I promised my wife we would be rich when I came home. I aim to keep that promise," Mr Brannigan chimed in.

These times were not going to get easier. Everything they said was true, but they forgot one important thing.

Chapter 58- On The Way Home

Mr. Biggs rode swiftly back to the wagons. "Only just ahead is the pass to Bidwell Bar. You young ones keep your wits. And you ladies stay close to your wagons.

Remember what I said this is a town of men. I mean only men, except for those ladies of ill reputation that occupy the saloons prying drinks from the poor souls who wish to squander their gold earnings. Stay with us and do not leave the train. Don't speak with anyone! Do you all understand? I will not have any more casualties on this train."

He rode off to make sure the road going into Bidwell Bar was clear and free from drunkards, freeloaders and highwaymen.

Bidwell Bar was a corrupt and free spirited settlement of miners, saloon keepers, thieves, and fortune seekers by any means possible. There were more saloons in Bidwell Bar than any town in the territory. The town actually boasted that they had twelve saloons and places of entertainment, and other buildings with such cavorting associations. The place was only just a few hundred yards long, lined with tents as resident housing, a few actual wooden buildings, and a few places that were in process of being built. All of which would take a mans toils and free him from both his money and his stresses, all for a very high price. Bidwell Bar was not a place for any man to stop or even think about raising his family. This was a hole in the ground that was said to be the entrance to hell itself and whoever ventured into it, for any amount of time, would surely be grabbed by the devil and held with a strong grip by the iniquities of the life style that were here.

"I will stay close at point and we will drive straight through. No stopping. Men, have your firearms at hand!" Mr. Biggs was strict on this instruction. He was not going to allow any of us to get stopped or delayed by anyone or any means. He had taken us on as if we were his very own children, and nothing was going to harm us.

"Young ladies, you get inside your wagons and you stay there. If you can stand to be silent for the ride, do it. Be as quiet as you can. All right now, rig your teams and let's go."

The wagons were rigged, and after a long three days of lifting with jacks and tackle again to put the wheels back on every one of them. The belongings that were still useable were placed back into the wagons and the teams were harnessed up. Everyone took a big long deep breath and sighed. Then Gridley Biggs took point and with everyone lined up in single file they were off into a world of who knows what. It sounded like Mr. Biggs had experienced this place first hand. What better way to know a place than to have someone guide you through who has been there.

Mr. Biggs being a staunch man of high character was never one to tell about his wild days or about what he had done as a carousing young man. You could say he was one to learn a lesson well taught and pass it on when he could. You might say this is why he became a wagon master. No one ever questioned his integrity, we were just very glad he was the one who stuck with us these many miles.

The pass was slippery from watery muddy holes and wheel rutted potholes. Tracked over and over with mule tracks, horse shoes, worn out boots from the miners, this pass was the only one that gave our teams any inkling of trouble.

They lost footing and fell slightly. Struggling to keep their footing with each step. Members of the families were pushing the wagons to help the teams get each wagon up and over that pass.

To go only a few miles it took the better part of the day. Five miles can prove itself a rugged road when it wants.

When they all arrived at the top, the train stopped. Everyone looked over a grand and vast valley of clear green and amber yellow landscape. They saw great buttes with more mountains in the distance, and looking both north and southward all they could see for miles was more miles.

" Hey! Look over here!" One man called out.

On a northern overlook towards a high ridge that ran next to the Feather River, grand forests of trees with intermixed shrubs, and scrub oaks, we saw two small settlements. One, further up than the first.

"That is where you folks want to go, Jacob. That is your new home. You have no concerns about civility up there. Families there are friendly and the ground very grassy, perfect for a new homestead. They have not forgotten their roots. They are good and friendly folks. You can farm, forest, and mine if you have a mind to. It has everything you asked about."

Jacob Summers shook Mr. Biggs hand firmly, and smiled, "Thank you." Jacob turned and walked back to the family wagon.

"Isobel asked, "What did Mr Biggs say, Jacob?"

Jacob could not help but smile as he took Isobel by her hand and pointed towards the foothills.

"Mr Biggs said that is where we will build your new front porch."

Chapter 59 - Goodbye Mr. Biggs

"You all come on now. We have a good half days ride ahead of us and we have not got time to stop and look-see all about. We still have to get through to Bidwell Bar without trouble. You children pay a mind to what I said now. Do you remember?"

Mr. Biggs was getting anxious. It seemed like he had a hankering to get somewhere special and could not get there fast enough. But, he knew we were his responsibility first thing.

Bidwell Bar was a raucous miners camp, and the wagon train had to travel through it.

The carousing that went on there was famous throughout the entire western region, and we were about to go into what was known as "the most corrupt town in all of California.

"Children, stay close and quiet in the wagons. Ladies, you climb aboard your wagons and stay put. There will be no getting off here for supplies. There is another town just over the rise and a few miles south of here called Ophir City. We can get supplies there. They won't be any less in cost, but they are friendlier in that town. Just keep going through and we will be to Ophir City in a couple of hours."

We headed down the grade from that beautiful lookout point that showed us the entire valley. It was so open and the green areas were dotted with places that looked like lakes and the buttes that rose up high in the near distance stood there like giants guardians. It was a grand sight.

Slowly the wagons, crawled down the trail. And with each sharp corner turn after sharp corner turn; going ever so carefully, so as not to tip over the wagons with us inside, and all the goods and belongings of others. One fall and that would be it; this was a steep and unforgiving road, as there was not much of a road much less that of an edge to the road.

The teams had to be driven with precision and care. At a snails pace in some parts was the way to travel. At one corner turn the road was crumbling away down a narrow trail. So narrow in fact that one wheel would hang in mid air as the wagon went around the corner. We would hang on sitting to the opposite side of the wagon so we wouldn't tip the wagon and be on our way down the hillside.

That must have been the most tense and scary few hours of out entire journey. Men were slipping and starting to slide down, and another would rush up to catch them in the nick of time! Thus saving them the fate of a long and painful fall in to the rocks far below.

We made it. Every one of us made it. When we arrived at the bottom, all the men, almost in unison, took out their kerchiefs and wiped their brows and then sat down to regain their breath. The children had never wanted to get out of the wagon so much.

"I think I will walk for a while now Mama." Katherine said.

"Me, too. I feel like I have just been tumbled about in some washtub laundry. Now I know what the clothes feel like when I wash them," Katey said rubbing the sore muscles she had gotten from the ride down.

"I thought it was fun," Jakie said.

"You are such a boy sometimes, Jacob junior," Katherine said. "Mama you should have seen him. He was hanging on for dear life. He would not let go of either of us. He was hanging on so tightly his knuckles were white. Every time we went around one of those sharp corners he would…"

"Alright, alright. That's enough now, Katherine. I heard him while I was hanging on too. That was a scary time for us all," Isobel said.

Things quieted down and everyones wits were back among them. Bidwell Bar was just ahead.

You could hear the noise from the stamp mills

grinding out the days gold findings and men yelling back and forth from the miner's camps.

Now, we had to go through this mess. With Mr Biggs help, we were on the way. Bidwell Bar, here we come.

To our surprise, it was considerably quiet. We could only speculate that the men who did most of the carousing were at the mines or claims and that was why the town was quiet. What luck we all thought. This isn't bad at all.

"Just keep em going!" Mr. Biggs called out. "We'll have no trouble today."

Everyone who was driving a wagon looked from side to side as the piloted their wagon, looking to see if anyone was even thinking of approaching. It was not as bad as Mr Biggs said it would be. There was not a soul, at least not very many in the town. Thank goodness!

The train made its way out of Bidwell Bar safely and quietly. Then another hour passed and another and we were in Ophir City. Mr. Biggs told us to gather at the main square for a meeting.

We all met, wagons and all. Mr Biggs had something important to tell us.

"Folks we have been through so much together.

I feel I know you all pretty well. After all the dust and rainstorms we've been through, and the attacks of wild animals and the new friends we have all made, I feel I have new family, but I am afraid this is where I must leave you now.

I have a dream too. I told myself this would be my last train. It is time for me to settle in and see what I can do with my hands other than hold reins and shoot. I wish you all the very best. I want you all to know this: anytime you need something, I won't be far off. I found myself a spread about ten miles south of here. Pretty nice too. Good farm land, and plenty of space to raise a few hundred head of cattle and horses. Who knows, maybe I will even find myself a wife and have some children like you, Jacob. You all know where you are going from here. The roads will be easy ones. You all take care and thanks!"

Gridley Biggs shook everyone's hand, even Jakie's, small as they were. You could hear the sniffles start to come and the kerchiefs being blown into. It was a sort of sad time but a great farewell to a friend and hero. Without Gridley Biggs who knows where any of them would be right now.

Mr. Biggs rode off on his seventeen hands high horse towards the south waving goodbye without turning to face us.

A few moments passed when a man came out of the mercantile general store and walked over to us and asked.

"You folks from the Biggs Train?"

We all stood there very curious, wondering why he asked.

"Mr. Biggs said you might be needing some supplies over to the general store. He said to get everything you needed to set up house keeping at your new homestead. It's all paid in full. I am the merchant there and I will meet you over at the store when you folks are ready."

"Wait! You said it was all paid in full. How?" Ethan asked the shop keeper.

The man showed them a leather bag, and out from that bag was all the money they paid Mr. Biggs when they left from Garden City so many weeks ago.

Our eyes brightened. Many of the men took off their hats and scratched their heads.

"Well I'll be. He never let on."

Chapter 60- Katey Goes Home

"That's it, then," Ethan said.

The air was sadly quiet. The remaining citizens of the wagon train stood there. Some with their heads hung down, some with their kerchiefs out wiping their running noses and drying the tears that were flowing down their cheeks.

The women who had become sisters over the long journey were all hugging and trying to smile at the same time. They had all become family.

"Where will you go? Where are your headed? Will we ever see each other again?"

Mrs. Emry asked.

Isobel was weeping soft tears. She lifted her apron to dry them as the women comforted each other before they all said their goodbyes.

The men were all shaking hands and patting each others backs. With each solid handshake they in turn, gave each other a feeling of reassurance that if any one of them needed any help, all they had to do was let it be known, via the crow path, and they would be there to lend a hand.

Somewhere down deep though, they all knew they might not ever see one another again.

"Where abouts you headed Jacob?" Ethan Emry asked.

"We are headed towards a place called Dogtown. It is somewhere on the ridge north of here, about 20 miles. We have a days ride around that table mountain, and just on the other side, I have been told, is where we want to go. It is an area with plenty of water and plenty of forest to make our new home. It will take some time and lots of patience to make it the way we want it to be. The very first thing I have to do is build a cabin to get us through the winter. I think I will take some of that money and buy us a wood stove to help keep the cold away."

"Sounds like the thing to do," Ethan added." We are going to the valley a fair piece north of there. It is a small town that runs right next to the Sacramento. Good farm land there, Mr. Emry said.

The families headed to the general store and got everything they thought they might need for the long months ahead. Plenty of flour, sugar, salt: all the staples for keeping the foodstuffs preserved. Then a few bolts of cloth and some

thread and new needles to keep them clothed and warm. Some ammunition for the rifles and pistols. A new sharpening stone for the axes and knives. Some even bought new pairs of shoes and boots. They had plum worn out the ones they started out with. Finally, one new wood-burning stove bought by the Summers family.

So, there they all were, one more handshake, and one more hug. The children gave each other special things they owned, a special toy or doll. A knife or kerchief, even a book or two.

They all waved goodbye like they did so many times before to friends along the trail this was different, the trip was almost over and done. There was an air of anxious wonder in each of them.

"Well, we made it to California," Jacob said. "I knew we could make it."

Isobel just smiled at her husband. The children walked along side their father and held his arm. Little Emily was on the seat of the wagon sitting next to Katey, holding her hand.

"Oh my, there is getting to be a chill in the air," Isobel said. "I think I'll get my shawl. Katherine you should get yours too."

"I'll get them," Katey said.

"Are you sure, child? Do you know where they are?" Isobel asked.

"Yes I know. They are in the large trunk with the leather straps. Would you take Emily, Katherine?

I will get the shawls?" Katey said.

Katey climbed into the back of the wagon and was trying to get the trunk open without disturbing too much of the other goods and belongings.

"Look, Papa, Zachary Emry gave me this sling shot. We traded. I gave him my pocketknife. Look, see, it works too," Jakie demonstrated.

Jakie launched a single small dried pea which held enough velocity and distance to strike one of the oxen on the rump causing the team to bolt, and with as much speed as an oxen can go made them jerk suddenly and began to run.

"Jacob Junior! Get after them, boy! Isobel where is Katey? Boy, if we lose that team it is your hide for sure!" Jacob shouted.

Jakie and Jacob ran after the team, not remembering that Katey was still being bounced about inside the wagon. "Help! Help Me!" Katey screamed.

The wagon was not slowing and the team was going full steam ahead as if they had the devil himself chasing them.

HELP! HELP! HELP!

Jacob did his best to catch up the team when in the near distance he saw the wagon hit a deep hole They all watched the wagon flip over and come to a heavy crash………………..

Katey awoke with a loud THUD. She found herself on her bedroom floor on her hands and knees, and very out of breath. She had fallen out of bed.

All was quiet. All was well, except for a bump on her forehead. She was by herself with just her stuffed animals on her bed and the beginnings of her genealogy outline for her report. There was no oxen team, no covered wagon, and no people. Her bedroom was completely quiet, just slight breeze coming through her bedroom window.

She was on her carpet-covered floor in just her pajamas. She sat up and looked around her room. On her shelves was the covered wagon replica she bought to help with her report and photos that she found on the internet from the Smithsonian Museum web site.

With a burst of excitement Katey ran downstairs with her report in hand.

"Grandma, Grandma! It was true! Everything you told me was true. They did have a have a hard time getting here and they did meet Indians and they did have trouble along the way!"

"Wait a minute, young lady what are you talking about?" Grandma asked.

"The pioneers. Our ancestors. The people you told me about last night. You know the Summers family! My great great grandparents and your grandparents. You were exactly right. I knownow! I went with them all the way from Minnesota to here. I rode all the way with them," Katey said.

"I think you need to sit down and rest. You have quite a big bump on your head. Are you all right?"

"Yes, I am fine. I can rest later. I have a lot of work to do. Wait! My genealogy report! I have to do my report. Wait! The shawl. I was getting a shawl. It was hand made by Grandma Isobel. It is blue with a fringe of yellow. She used it to wrap herself when she got chilly. She kept it in a large trunk with leather straps. They brought it with them from Garden City.

"How do you know about the trunk I keep in the attic? Its' full of old things I have inherited. That shawl is in there," Grandma asked and wondered what was going on with her granddaughter.

"Hey, Grandma, I have never asked you this before, but, what is your name? I have always just called you grandma," Katey asked.

"My name has always been Emily. I was named after..."

Katey happily interrupted, "I know. You were named after Emily Summers who almost died two times on the journey to California. Once of cholera, and once of the croup."

"Oh my goodness! No time for breaksfast now. I have to get my report done. Can I look at the things later?"

As Katey started to leave, she stopped and turned to her grandma. "Thanks Grandma for giving me this heritage. This is so great! This is so cool! I'll be in my room if anyone needs me."

Katey ran up stairs jabbering a mile a minute as if

she were having a conversation with a million people

She sat down at her desk and began to write her heritage report like her hands were filled with electricity.

Then, in the living room, an overwhelming quiet filled the air. It was as if a stampede of a thousand buffalo had just gone through the house, and then simply vanished leaving no sound at all. A ten year old whirlwind had come and gone in a matter of seconds.

Grandma and Jakie just looked at each other in amazement.

"Wow!" Jakie said. "Sometimes, I think my sister is nuts!"

Jakie turned to walk away, and there, hanging from his back pocket, was an old slingshot with the initials Z.E. carved into the handle, big as life.

Grandma caught notice of it, held a finger to her lips and whispered, "Where in the world?" She shook her head and said, "Nah, it couldn't be."

A Word of Thanks!

A special word of thanks and appreciation…

It is the greatest feeling to complete a story that so many have enjoyed. It is only because of the many resources I have been fortunate to get to know and glean my research from, that this somewhat factual historical story of the Summers family's adventure to the Butte County California area.

In the research that was done to write, what started out as The Feather River Adventure, I wish to thank the docents of the Gold Nugget museum in Paradise, California, The Oroville Dam Regional Park Museum the Plumas County Museum and information center with special thanks to the Butte County Historical Society, I would also like to thank The Smithsonian Museum. The Nakahara and Hiroshi families of San Francisco. The cities far too numerous to mention and the many others that no longer exist along this journey. The many historical forts now national parks along these famous pioneer trails. Especially the Humboldt Trail Historical Society.

The Omaha Indian Tribe in Nebraska, the University of Nebraska, the many historians, and the descendants of the families I was able to contact throughout the country who helped me give chase and capture to a story that might have been lost.

Thanks Very Much
Author T.E. Watson